The Tao of Montessori

The Tao of Montessori

◆

Reflections on Compassionate Teaching

Catherine McTamaney

iUniverse Star
New York Lincoln Shanghai

The Tao of Montessori
Reflections on Compassionate Teaching

iUniverse Star
an iUniverse, Inc. imprint

iUniverse books may be ordered through booksellers or by contacting:

iUniverse
2021 Pine Lake Road, Suite 100
Lincoln, NE 68512
www.iuniverse.com
1-800-Authors (1-800-288-4677)

ISBN-13: 978-1-58348-298-8 (pbk)
ISBN-13: 978-0-595-86544-4 (ebk)
ISBN-10: 1-58348-298-9 (pbk)
ISBN-10: 0-595-86544-5 (ebk)

Printed in the United States of America

For My Children

Gratitude

No love or friendship can ever cross our path without affecting us in some way forever.

—Muriac

I have been dearly blessed to have had more remarkable teachers than one person deserves and more than one person could ever list. Sometimes, we don't realize how great the lessons were, or how influential our teachers were, until long after we have left their care. I am grateful to the many teachers, those who called themselves Montessorians and those who did not, whose influence still drives me.

Just as there are far too many to count, there are some whose touch was so profound that it cannot go unmentioned. The first of these, of course, is Amelia, whose commitment to Montessori opened my life to this practice when I was a young child and who continues to push me toward a deeper understanding of my purpose, even as an adult. My work, as a student, teacher, and mother, is your legacy.

I offer my gratitude, too, to those superlative Montessorians whose lives serve as my model. I hope one day to earn the joyful welcoming of Anthonita Porta, the gracious wisdom of Sighle Fitzgerald, and the indefatigable drive of Jane Dutcher. Thank you, humbly, for the torches you each held high for me. I am still finding my way down the path, but it is along trails you forged.

Without the generous support of the American Montessori Society and the Ursula Thrush Peace Seed Grant, this book may never have made it from my heart to my laptop. Ursula Thrush's vision of peace through education and her belief in the impact of small actions have helped me to realize this was work worth doing. I am thankful to my colleagues at AMS who read the early essays and agreed. I pray that these simple musings may help to spread Ursula's work even further.

The lion's share of these essays was written at the University School of Nashville, a community as overflowing with unwitting Montessorians as I ever have found. I am deeply grateful for the use of my perch in the Zendlovitz Reading Area, both for the peaceful surroundings it provided me and for the glimpse of students and teachers, young and old, engaged in confident and esteemed collaboration. David Plummer's inspired architecture was my prepared environment. I hope these essays, like his design, are both grounded and soaring.

I am always, if sometimes silently, grateful to my husband, Bryan, for his humble simplicity, ceaseless patience, and enduring compassion.

Finally, to the many Montessori teachers with whom I have laughed and cried, who have shared with me their successes and comforted me in my failures, and to the many more Montessori teachers who continue this great work with vigor and faith, thank you and *namaste.*

A Note to the Reader

The *Tao Te Ching* was originally written down sometime in the fourth century BCE. Or perhaps the fifth century BCE. Or possibly the sixth. Tradition says that it was written by Lao-tzu, a teacher of Confucius. Other legends attribute the thoughts to Lao-tzu but the writing to his followers. Other stories claim that Lao-tzu was an archivist for the emperor who was not permitted to leave his post until he had written down all his knowledge, which he did shortly before he disappeared. Still others claim that Lao-tzu never existed at all. While there is little agreement about the history of these verses or their author, they remain a powerful spiritual guide. They have been translated around the world and interpreted by other authors throughout their history.

As it is read today, the *Tao Te Ching* is a series of eighty-one verses. *The Tao of Montessori* takes the same structure, relying upon the corresponding chapters of the *Tao Te Ching* for thematic motivation. Like its inspiration, this book is not intended to be read linearly. Pick it up. Read a little. Put it down for a while. Visit and revisit so long as it speaks to you.

Montessori wrote, "We are the sowers—our children are those who reap. We labor so that future generations will be better and nobler than we are."

Good labor to you.

1

The tao that can be described
Is not the eternal Tao.
The name that can be spoken
Is not the eternal Name.

"What is Montessori?"

As educators, we are asked that question often by parents, other teachers, and people on the street. We ask ourselves, "What is Montessori?" every time we choose a new material for the classroom or attend a professional development workshop or try to improve our practice.

Perhaps we're asking the wrong question.

The idea that there is *a* "Montessori," one way to respond, one way to prepare our classrooms, one training program, one school day, one magic combination of ingredients that makes a classroom or a school a "real" Montessori program separates us from our authentic work. When we ask this question, we focus on ourselves and on our interpretation of the philosophy, on territory rather than on children. We distance ourselves from other educators from whom we might learn. We make ourselves elite, unique, and apart. In short, we make "Montessori" a noun instead of a verb.

When we live Montessori, we recognize that Montessori classrooms take on a thousand different embodiments, from school to school and from year to year. What makes a Montessori program is that intangible, unnamable breath that loves unconditionally the children in its care, that accepts and propels without judgment, that seeks to find commonalities to unite rather than to separate. It is a peacefulness and a peace seeking that goes beyond political affiliations and school accreditations.

When we objectify Montessori, we set an unattainable goal. We visit other schools and wish our classrooms worked so well. We attend conferences with the hope of becoming more Montessori. We criticize each other, even if only in our own heads, as not being Montessori enough. We send the message to young practitioners that there is one goal to strive for, that after enough years or enough practice or enough reading or enough essay writing, they will finally be "Montessori teachers." In doing so, we emphasize what we promise our children we will never demand of them: product over process.

When we realize that Montessori is a verb, an action and not a thing, we grant ourselves the grace to grow as teachers. We grant ourselves the union of community with other educators. We grant ourselves the day instead of the year-end. When we realize that Montessori cannot be named or labeled or identified but only acted out, we cast the spell.

I beseech you, do not go around speaking of an educational method that has convinced you, nor of having studied the way to make culture for children easy, universal, and attractive. Therefore speak to everyone of the child and of his secret; unveil the truth; reveal the powers of this "spiritual embryo" of the human soul; proclaim him for what he is; the father of man, the builder of humanity, the creative and transforming energy which can act on the hearts of men and can offer new elements for the solution of social problems.

—Maria Montessori

2

When people see things as beautiful,
Ugliness is created.
When people see things as good,
Evil is created.

Montessori observed the phenomena of "normalization," that condition during which children showed their true nature, a peacefulness, a calm, an industriousness that has come to be surprising in young children. We seek normalization in our classrooms. We discuss children as not yet normalized. We admire the normalized child who was such a handful before.

By focusing, though, on the goal of the normalized child, we distance ourselves from the children at hand. Each child in our classrooms comes to us perfect, and it is our obligation to treat the child with the same love and reverence when his or her behavior is challenging as we do this idealized normalized child. Consider the normalized child who suddenly suffers a trauma, such as an ill family member or the parents' divorce. We grant this child more grace, because we have seen this child as normalized, than we do the child who has yet to overcome the simpler, hidden stresses of children's lives. We are more forgiving. We are more compassionate. We have loved the normalized child entirely, and because we have loved her, we hurt with her and for her.

Each child deserves that same forgiveness, that same compassion; for the work each child accomplishes on the path to adulthood is exactly the work that child is to do. Montessori warned us that we could not do the work of becoming on the child's behalf. We see children who, it seems, have everything, and it is difficult not to hold their life's status against them when their behavior challenges us. We become angry with their parents for spoiling them or for not doing just as we have directed. We are frustrated that they don't respond as quickly, that they are not served by the materials we have chosen for them. And in our judgment, we separate ourselves even further. It is only through empathy that we can understand the child's life. It is only through compassion that we can serve her. We must look at the child who is standing in front of us (or lying on the ground screaming in front of us!) and see the child who is yet to come. We revere the child for her potential. We respect her for her promise. While bearing witness to the normalized child serves us well, encourages us to continue to do this work, and gives foundation to our accomplishment as teachers, sometimes the most important work we do is for the child we never see change.

If we have neither sufficient experience nor love to enable us to distinguish the fine and delicate expressions of the child's life, if we do not know how to respect them, then we perceive them only when they are manifested violently.

—Maria Montessori

3

For those who practice not-doing,
Everything will fall into place.

Remember the three roles of the Montessori teacher? We are taught to be servants to the child, carefully preparing the environment. We are taught to be scientists, observing the child at work, in order more carefully to respond to the child's unique and individual needs. Finally, we are taught to be saints. But how? How do we "do" saintliness?

We are saintly when we are still, when we do not seek to change or to affect or to modify or to improve any other human around us but when, in our stillness, we accept. We are saintly when we mirror for the child the wondrous balance between accepting ourselves completely while still engaging life. We are saintly when we stop mopping up, following children with brooms and brushes to maintain our perfectly prepared environments, and instead observe the tiny miracles that unfold at every moment in our classrooms. A child discovers the sound of beads crashing. Do we respond by chiding? Do we draw attention to the disruption? We are saintly when we acknowledge the cacophonous new noise before we help the child to figure out how not to do it again! We are saintly when we recognize that each unfolding moment in each child's life is lost the minute it exists, and thus live presently with the children in our care.

We are saintly, too, when we model compassion and grace. Montessorians present lessons in grace and courtesy with expertise ... how often do we apply those lessons to ourselves? Do we find failure in our colleagues when their challenges make more work for us? Do we find comfort in making ourselves elite from other schools when their interpretation serves children differently than we would? We are saintly when we do for each other, as adults, what we hope the children will learn to do in the microcosm of the classroom. We are saintly when we acknowledge that, like the child, each adult we encounter is doing the very best he can with the tools he has and the life he has led. We are saintly when we commit ourselves to teaching through example, when we focus on the planks in our own eyes and, by doing so, help those around us to see.

Perhaps the reason we focus on the roles of scientist and servant is because it is in these expressions that we find the concrete, manageable elements of Montessori. We know how to sweep. We can prepare materials as our manuals show us. We can rely on forms and methods for observation. The fact that there are no *rules* for saintliness is the precise reason we need so diligently to pursue it. We can never assess how well we have served the spirits of the children in our care, and so we must maintain that as the first goal of our classrooms. If it is delegated to holidays and birthdays, if it becomes an afterthought of our teaching, we are certain to have failed. It is only by prioritizing the spiritual lives of our children, by affirming ourselves as spiritual models, that we can hope to scratch the nose of saintliness.

The child is truly a miraculous being, and this should be felt deeply by the educator.

—Maria Montessori

4

The Tao is like an empty container:
It can never be emptier and can never be filled.
Infinitely deep, it is the source of all things.

We have been given a gift in the children we serve. How grateful are we? We are able to share in the lives of these children, to observe and to participate in the unwinding expression of their individuality. How often, though, do we stop? Stop teaching. Stop talking. Stop fretting. Stop scrubbing. Stop complaining. Stop doing, and be with the children?

It is easy to be consumed by the elements of our classrooms we can control. We can be sure of the plans in our plan book. We can practice presentations so they are perfectly replicable each time. We can control our dress. We can clean the environment. All these things are important, but none of them is as important as the love we offer these children. When we are loving to our children, these other elements become an expression of that love rather than a substitution for it.

Who is "the child" Montessori talks about so frequently? Each child is "the child." The one who misbehaves is "the child." The one who returns each material with exactness and care is "the child." The one whose parents disagree with us is "the child." The one whose parents volunteer and donate and offer and support is "the child." The one who pushes on the playground. The one who just can't seem to get to the toilet on time. The one who pours beans down the drain. The one who wiggles incessantly at nap time. The one who makes our hearts smile with the gift of a ragged dandelion. The one who thanks us for small kindnesses. The one who reminds us of our children or our parents or ourselves in a smaller body. When we recognize the transcendental child in the one who is right in front of us, it is impossible not to be loving. It is impossible not to be grateful.

Each child is "the child." Each child is filled with the unknowable, unpredictable greatness of potential. Each child promises a redemption from the culture we've created, from the hate and anger and war and hurt that surround us as adults. If we are able to recognize each child as "the child," perhaps we may serve the child more fully. Seeing each child as worthy of immeasurable respect raises the stakes … it forces us to focus on the things we can't control. In doing so, it forces us to take responsibility for unpredictable outcomes. When things go wrong, we can't blame the children anymore. When things go well, we can't take credit. We are left in a crooked place of gratitude, grateful to the unknowable element of the child who has left us elated or exhausted or both.

It is necessary, then, to give the child the possibility of developing according to the laws of his nature, so that he can become strong, and, having become strong, can do even more than we dared hope for him.

—Maria Montessori

5

The space between Heaven and Earth is like a bellows:
It is empty, yet has not lost its power.
The more it is used, the more it produces:
The more you talk of it, the less you comprehend.

What were the questions that plagued you during your Montessori training? Did you question the precise placement of your fingers on a material? Or the proper sequence of presentations? Did you obsess over the exact dimensions of the teacher-made materials you so painstakingly produced? Did you hear the voice quietly asking in the background of that cacophony, "How will I become a Montessorian?"

That is the question hardest answered and the one that we so often ignore in exchange for more manageable tasks. The simple answer is "time." The tasks of training are important. Indeed, they are critical. But the most important ingredient in our own success is time. The only person who can teach you to teach is the child in front of you (and the child behind him and the child beside her and the child waiting around the corner!) and it is only through the lived failures of our experience that we become teachers.

So what, then, in the meantime? Do we fumble around, pretending to know what we're doing until we actually do? Do we put on a good show, do the things we see other good teachers do, until somehow it begins to feel right?

Yup.

Find the people you know know Montessori, not just the ones who call themselves Montessorians but those individuals who seem to know how to speak with children with some magic, the ones who children seem to hear differently. All the precision of practiced time with the materials is useless without that magic. But that magic can be emulated, and reproduced,

9

more easily than you might think. Because Montessori works when you do it; even if you don't know why you do it, it works. And upon that success, more grows. Eventually, it becomes second nature, but in the meantime, it may be the only way to keep afloat. How many Montessori teachers do you know who believed so deeply in this method but left the practice nonetheless, victims of their own restless standard setting? Talk to the teachers who stay. Ask them about the struggles of their first years.

Find companionship in expertise, and expertise in time.

There is in the soul of a child an impenetrable secret that is gradually revealed as it develops.

—Maria Montessori

6

It is called the Great Mother
Because it gives birth to Heaven and Earth.
It is like a vapor,
Barely seen but always present.
Use it effortlessly.

From classroom to classroom, school to school, we argue over what "real" Montessori looks like. We are critical of others who do it differently, or unsure of ourselves when we struggle to do it right.

We are better to focus on the things that unite us, particularly in this very difficult work, than to compare ourselves endlessly against a nonexistent model. Here is what we share: We believe that children are inherently wise. We believe that, given an environment free of adult obstacle, children's essential nature is protected and propelled. We believe that children want to learn and that they can do so in an environment swimming in peace. We believe that one child's success does not impede another's. Each classroom that holds these beliefs as its core continues to be Montessori.

In our shared history, our great challenge has not been in serving the children in our care but in serving the adults who walk beside us. Imagine, then, a Montessori community with these shared beliefs: We believe other Montessorians are inherently wise. We believe that, given an environment free of our obstacles, other Montessorians' essential nature is protected and propelled. We believe that other Montessorians want to learn and that they can do so in an environment swimming in peace. We believe that one Montessorian's success does not impede another's.

When we have committed ourselves to the ideals of Montessori, when we have firmly planted ourselves upon the humanitarian ground this method sows, we are obligated to offer the same grace to other Montessorians that we offer to the children before us. We have chosen a most difficult work, and we have surrounded ourselves, by the very nature of Montessori, with a group of people who came to this method because they each individually thought they could serve children differently, better than the norm. What a party! We have invited our most headstrong, opinionated friends to dine together and expected an easy meal! Once we acknowledge, though, that each of our colleagues has chosen this most difficult work for the same core reasons we have—that is, to serve children—perhaps we might find compassion for one another's differences rather than condemnation. So long as children are born their own individuals, so long as we hold fast the belief that each child is unique and perfect, we are obligated to massive and diverse incarnations of the method. When we trade re-union for pride, we will have respected the multitude of worlds of Montessori, spinning around the multitude of children they serve. And although we still may not agree on the menu, we can disagree in a way that still offers a place at the table.

Whoever touches the life of the child touches the most sensitive point of a whole which has roots in the most distant past and climbs toward the infinite future.

—Maria Montessori

7

The Master puts herself last;
And finds herself in the place of authority.
She detaches herself from all things;
Therefore she is united with all things.
She gives no thought to self.
She is perfectly fulfilled.

When teachers answer the question, "Why did you decide to be a teacher?" most answers include some variation of "Because I love children." What a remarkable foundation, so unlikely in other professions, to feel passionately about the work we do, so much so that we are often willing to do it for little pay and little recognition. Teaching, for most of us, satisfies some inner drive, compelled by our individual relationships with the children for whom we care. Perhaps a more informative question to ask, though, would be, "Why do you love children?"

It is within the answers to this question that we find the more difficult obstacles to conquer, those parts of our relationships with children that make our work about us instead of about them. Do we love children, or do we love the way children make us feel about ourselves? Montessori calls for a selfless commitment to the child. Within that commitment, there is little space for the self-gratifying pursuit of acceptance, of approval, of love *from* the children. When we are in service to the child, we are so in sacrifice of our own fulfillment. Knowing, then, that a child "likes me" or indeed "loves me" becomes far less important than knowing that we have observed the child and prepared the environment most appropriate for that child's development.

When we disconnect our work with the children from our personal need for validation, we are able to better serve the children in our care. We can focus more precisely on their needs, because our own are not intermingled to muddy the waters. We can observe children outside of our biases, prepare for them outside of our own agendas, and respect them for themselves instead of for whom they make us feel we are. Being loving toward children is in itself a validation of our lovingness.

Are we, then, to view teaching as burdensome? Are we to abandon the personal fulfillment we feel in our practice? Of course not! All teaching, and Montessori in particular, draws us because of the pieces of our own hearts it fills. Were we not to find the completion in our work, we would leave it. But serving children first and distancing our needs is uniquely successful in Montessori. The qualities we identify of the normalized child show themselves when the child is free of all adult obstacles, even those that are seemingly loving. Our classrooms become more functional, healthier, and more balanced when we remove our own needs from the children's. The children in our care perpetuate peacefulness, intrinsic motivation, and community when we stop asking them to satisfy us and allow them instead to follow their own inner guides. Authentic, selfless love for the child revolves around an authentic, self-love ... if we accept ourselves sufficiently that our need for acceptance is not demanded of the children, we are able to offer unconditional love to them. Indeed, the outcome is clear. The child who has been loved without expectation of reimbursement is able to offer that to others. The child whose acceptance is tied to his or her fulfillment of someone else's needs is taught a much different lesson about the nature of love.

Knowing what we must do is neither fundamental nor difficult, but to comprehend which presumptions and vain prejudices we must rid ourselves of in order to be able to educate our children is most difficult.

—Maria Montessori

8

The location makes the dwelling good.
Depth of understanding makes the mind good.
A kind heart makes the giving good.
Only when there is no competition
Will we all live in peace.

It feels often that there are too many things to do in our classrooms. There are always more materials to prepare, more observations to accomplish, more to do for the children and the environment. Are the baseboards clean? Are there chips in the paint? Is the tray the perfect shade of blue? We can make ourselves wild with the busyness of teaching, particularly in a philosophy that emphasizes the prepared environment.

Our lives are gelatinous. We spread to fill whatever container we are in. Every shelf ends up filled, every corner complete. Think, though, about the Nido, the environment for the tiniest children we serve. Our infant spaces are simple, absent of overwhelming color. The few items that are present are carefully chosen. They are beautiful. They are complete. They are simple. At what point, between infancy and early childhood, do we change route? Does the introduction of the sandpaper letters to the environment necessarily mean we must also have twenty-six books on the reading shelf? Does the existence of thousand cubes mean we must have thousands of other things to accompany them as well? When we overwhelm our environments with things, even carefully prepared, beautifully maintained things, we overwhelm the children as well.

Keep it simple.

Perfection does not come in the number of things in the environment. It comes from the choosing of items that, like the materials originally designed for our classrooms, have only a single purpose. Think of the Montessori materials. They are simple, unembellished. They know where they came from—the lines of the wood boxes visible, the grain of the tree apparent. They do one thing extraordinarily well. The child finds the beauty inherent in the simplest of items, staring intently at the indentations in a tiny seed, eagerly watching lint float to the ground. Follow that instinct of the child. Allow your classroom to be simple, complete, and beautiful.

In the simplicity of the Montessori materials, there are endless possibilities. In the simplicity of the child's mind there even more. Clutter the classroom, clutter the child with stuff, and you have filled an open pathway with obstacles. We should offer the child tools to see the path more clearly instead of cement to close it up.

It may be said that that we acquire knowledge by using our minds; but the child absorbs knowledge directly into his psychic life.

—Maria Montessori

9

When you have accomplished your goal
Simply walk away.

Teachers of the very young are a curious sort. In some ways, we are the most generous, the most selfless, the most giving. We accept and work with children who drive other teachers mad. We embrace the extraordinary individualism that makes each child wondrously unique. In other ways, though, we can be most selfish, most egocentric. We love to teach because "the children love us." We enjoy the unconditional love our children offer. In short, we teach because it makes us feel good about ourselves. Children offer a captive and absolute audience for those of us who seek the stage.

There is no great sin in this ... if we didn't enjoy our work, if it wasn't personally fulfilling, we would abandon it, physically or emotionally. But sometimes the emotional satisfaction of being with the child supercedes our practice as Montessorians. We trade children who are independent, self-reliant, and purposeful for those who make us feel more deeply loved. We hover and linger and hold too tightly, because it gives us security, rather than doing only what is needed, then moving away.

Remember the old story from training about the caterpillar, emerging into a butterfly. When the butterfly first emerges, it pumps its wings, over and over, moving essential fluids into the farthest nooks of its flight. The pumping is strenuous work for a newborn creature, and yet if a "helpful" human opens the butterfly's wings for it, the butterfly will never learn to fly. It is in the careful observation, and the respectful distance from the butterfly's work, that we are most supportive of its growth. When we intervene, when we act as though we understand more about this life than the life itself, we destroy it.

When we walk with an infant—helping the child by holding his hands above his head, carrying the child's weight for him—the child is taught to walk dependently, to reach up toward his parents rather than out for himself. The child toddles longer and that inherent ability to balance is taught right out of him. When we walk by his side, he learns to walk with us, rather than to depend upon us for his movement.

When we tell children, "Do this for me," "I would like you to …," "I need you to …," we likewise place the purpose of the work upon our own acceptance. The child is taught that work is tied to his teacher's approval. We take from him his own inherent motivation, his ability to work for the work's sake, and replace it with work for our own sake.

Do not erase the designs the child makes in the soft wax of his inner life.

—Maria Montessori

10

Giving birth and nourishing
Making without possessing,
Expecting nothing in return.
To grow, yet not to control:
This is the mysterious virtue.

Parents and teachers, come to Montessori for very many different reasons. The variety is illustrated in the number of diverse, sometimes diametrically opposed Montessori schools thriving in the same community. Is there a "hippie Montessori" school in your area? Is there the "Montessori prep school"? Is there the "Montessori-based" preschool? Or the one where the teachers "take the best of Montessori" and combine it with other ideas?

We know the strength of our academic materials, and so we expect advanced academic achievement from the child. We know the potential for peace in Montessori, so we are disappointed by the children who are not peaceful. We understand the community that can be developed in a Montessori classroom, so we are discouraged when the children are hurtful or exclusive with each other.

Our expectations speak louder than our words.

We appreciate the academics, so we emphasize that in our admissions programs and implementation of the method. And so we end up with a classroom with strong academics, because we and the parents are teaching the children that expectation. We value the peacefulness and self-direction, and so we attract teachers and parents who value the same. We end up with peaceful classrooms. We teach what we love. And so we get more of that in return.

When we are able to step back from our own expectations and view the classroom as the child does, with endless possibilities each equally valuable, we return to the natural state of the child. When we trust that each child, although different in his or her strengths, will nonetheless be remarkable, we find in each child that exceptionality. If we are able to put aside our desired outcomes and live and teach simply and lead without trying to control, we may surprise ourselves by better attaining the loftiest of our goals.

Education demands, then, only this: the utilization of the inner powers of the child for his own instruction.

—*Maria Montessori*

11

Thirty spokes are joined together in a wheel,
But it is the center hole
That allows the wheel to function.

Beyond our work to prepare the environment, there is that untouchable center around which all our preparations are designed. How quiet and solitary our classrooms are before the children arrive … likewise, how vibrant and unfettered they are when the children are unfolding within them.

We can build our classrooms, we can prepare the environment with precision and care, and we are still not responsible for the child's development. The only person who can take the credit for that work is the child. Our preparations are an effort to support, to reinforce the building the child is creating. We can offer materials, but we cannot construct the house.

This is frustrating sometimes. We want the child to learn a new skill on our time frame. We are daunted that this child cannot remember the letters we have reviewed day after day after day. And then, suddenly, the explosion! The child is reading, unassisted, and beyond what we thought he knew. We didn't change at all, but suddenly the child, through that unknowable, untouchable center, has made connections beyond what we were able to build and has come to a higher place without us. We shone our flashlights down the tunnel, to be sure, but the child walked alone into the sun.

There is a peace that comes to teachers who have learned to trust in that center hole, who have learned that the child's learning is beyond their own teaching. It is a combined relaxation of the pressures we put on ourselves, because we recognize that we are not ultimately responsible, and a heightening of the demands for the preparations we make, because we recognize that "but-for" symbiosis of our work. The child constructs on his own, with the blocks we offer him. We can step back from our own agendas and simultaneously respect more deeply the needs of the child.

Our goal is not so much the imparting of knowledge as the unveiling and developing of spiritual energy.

—*Maria Montessori*

12

Five colors blind the eye.
Five notes deafen the ear.
The Master acts on what she feels and not what she sees.
She shuns the latter, and prefers to seek the former.

How boring our classrooms are! No bright colors! No ball pits! Children sitting quietly, working attentively to only one thing at a time. Where is Barney? Where is Ronald McDonald? Don't we understand that children want to have *fun*?

Simple environments, few choices. Are these the qualities of a boring classroom? In Montessori, they are the cornerstones of the child's imagination. When we debate the role of fantasy in our classrooms, we come back to these real items, these few, orderly materials presented with such care. The child, who absorbs everything around her, is offered only those things that are real. In doing so, have we taken all the fun out? No. Rather, we have respected the inner vision of the child. By experiencing stimuli, colors, sounds, flavors in isolation instead of cacophony, the child observes the world around her and develops a more profound understanding of it than if we offered her syrupy "fun." The world is a symphony. Begin with a single note.

Our children come to us complete, accepting, peaceful, knowing, and we throw them into a world that is without reality. By protecting the child's understanding of reality, by presenting her with real concepts in isolation, we have preserved the child's inherent knowing. Watching a child at work in a Montessori classroom is like watching the truest prayer spoken. Peaceful concentration, joyful noise. The child, in offering her attention to the tiniest detail, respects the wonder of her world. She does not overlook the miraculous seed. She attends to the color of the rabbit's eyes. By protecting the space from too much color, too much noise, too much distraction, we preserve in the child the ability to wonder. We offer her the ability to hear each tone, to appreciate the complexity of the symphony by understanding first each simple sound.

It is almost possible to say that there is a mathematical relationship between the beauty of his surroundings and the activity of the child; he will make discoveries rather more voluntarily in a gracious setting than in an ugly one.

—Maria Montessori

13

Love the whole world as if it were your self;
Then you will truly care for all things.

We set such enormous expectations for ourselves, mirror the behavior of teachers whose behavior inspires us, and express such disappointment on the days when things go poorly.

Who are we, to expect perfection from ourselves? Why should we be more capable of perfection than we expect others to be? When we release ourselves from the expectation of perfection, we can be more accepting of others as well.

We ask the unattainable of ourselves because we want the best for ourselves. We want to be perfect teachers. We want to do things right the first time. We want not to have to face failure. Montessori, though, is about the process of learning, not the product. We must see ourselves as travelers on the same path as the children in our classroom. When we offer ourselves that same grace, we model it for the children. We can extend grace and forgiveness and authentic love to the children in our care because we have experienced it firsthand toward ourselves.

Likewise, when we appreciate that the world around us is a part of our essential life, we find ourselves capable of offering *metta,* or loving kindness, even to those parts of our lives that we would rather do without.

When you yell across the playground, your message is easily lost to the wind. When you calmly approach the child, whisper in his ear, your message is safe, intact, and received. When we accept the children as a part of ourselves, when we shorten the distance between our lives and theirs, we care for them in a more spiritually respectful manner, and we increase the quality of that care.

We strengthen our teaching and the lives of our children when we offer the same grace and acceptance to ourselves as to them, when we recognize that our failures are the lessons learned. Our lives, like the materials on the shelf, are self-correcting, if we pay close enough attention. Realize that the errors in our lives, like a mistake made with a material, is not our essence but a lesson to be learned in our own growth.

It is well to cultivate a friendly feeling towards error, to treat it as a companion inseparable from our lives, as something having a purpose which it truly has.

—Maria Montessori

14

Approach it and you will not see a beginning;
Follow it and there will be no end.
When we grasp the Tao of the ancient ones,
We can use it to direct our life today.

We are told often to "follow the child." What does that look like? Can we possibly follow *every* child? Won't we fall into utter chaos? What will happen to our lesson plans? What will happen to our control?

Following the child requires attention, observation, and a very intimate knowledge. In order to understand where she leads, following the child requires us to understand the child's motivations, her development, her fears, and her joys. A daunting task, perhaps so daunting that it becomes much easier to follow our manuals than the children before us. "Follow the child" becomes a slogan we pull out when we can't otherwise justify our teaching. "Follow the child" becomes how we defend our disconnection.

In our classrooms, we begin with the simple and move to the complex. We introduce children first to those things that are familiar before asking their imaginations to digest the foreign. The same strategy applies as we follow the child. Begin with the child with whom you are most familiar. Begin with the child you know best. Begin with the child you once were (and perhaps, at your most vulnerable or most comfortable, still are!). Push yourself to remember what drove you as a child, what frightened you or inspired you. Ask yourself how it felt to be a student to the teacher who terrified you and recall how the one who adored you made you feel. Consider how you may have behaved differently had it not been for those teachers, the ones who kept you in line and the ones who made you want to rebel. Follow first the compassion you would have had shown to yourself, if your voice had been able to be heard.

The children we serve have voices as quiet as ours once were. They may not be able to ask directly to be heard, but they will ask in as many different ways as their growing minds can imagine. They will ask for your observation by drawing attention to themselves, or ask you to look the other way by drawing none. When you can find yourself in the children in front of you, hearing their messages becomes easier. When the child ceases to be foreign to you, separate from you, an entity to be uncovered and dissected, when you see the misbehavior as a desperate message instead of an affront, you can offer the child the compassion you deserved in your own childhood.

Compassion is redemption.

We do not believe in the educative power of words and commands alone, but seek cautiously, and almost without the child's knowing it, to guide his natural activity.

—*Maria Montessori*

15

Who can be still
Until their mud settles
And the water is cleared by itself?
Can you remain tranquil until right action occurs by itself?

How many of us come to Montessori because we believe we have found "the way," then find ourselves losing faith when our anticipated successes don't happen quickly enough? We fear that the materials might not work, and so we supplement. We "enrich." New to the faith, we're not completely convinced of the ritual, so we carry with us the totems from our former lives, in handouts, paperwork, and forty-nine miniature frogs.

Montessori asks of us an enormous leap of faith. We cannot necessarily see the outcome of our work even over the course of a year. Sometimes, it is three years or more before the peaceful, focused classroom reveals itself. Why should we believe, in the meantime, that it really will come?

Find the ancient sages. Observe the teachers who have led a lifetime of Montessori practice and are still in the classroom, the ones whose love of children is apparent in every action, the ones who smile at the difficult child. If you have not yet experienced it yourself, surround yourself regularly with those who have.

Confidence is a skill like any other. Faith requires practice. When you doubt, model the patience you see in those mentors, but when you question, question. Acknowledge the fear so that you can overcome it. Assume of yourself the same that you assume of the children: they will need to see, feel, touch, smell, and hear the evidence before they will understand. Likewise, you need to experience the materials' success before you can be sure of your decision to put away the traditional substitutes. These trinkets, left over from our traditional teaching, obscure the view. They overshadow the beauty of the simple golden beads. A classroom filled with rubber and plastic interferes with the pleasure of wood, glass, and silk. We are left with bells and whistles instead of the mystic sound of sand and stone in a cylinder. You cannot truly believe in this method unless you have held the proof in your hand. That proof, though, cannot be offered in an environment that is filled with distractions.

Our lives are filled with doubt. So be it. There was a time when you questioned whether your tiny legs would hold you upright. There was a time, too, when you had to let go of your mother's hand. We know how much longer it takes for the infant to stand when we walk him with arms above his head, when we leave him to artificial supports. We don't abandon the child to a bouncy seat or baby swing. We stay nearby, we comfort the child when he falls, and we recognize when we must move away. Learning to teach in this way requires a new set of legs. If you are toddling, surround yourself with comforting hands. If you are running already, offer your hands out to the wobbly teachers around you. Have confidence that you have within you the tools to stand, to walk, to dance.

The adult ought never to mold the child after himself, but should leave him alone and work always from the deepest comprehension of the child himself.

—*Maria Montessori*

16

If you can empty your mind of all thoughts
Your heart will embrace the tranquility of peace.
Watch the workings of all creation,
But contemplate their return to the source.
All creatures in the universe
Return to the point where they began.

Watch the turmoil of beings ... what better description for the Montessori classroom during that sacred period we call "false fatigue"! We see the chaos. We know our classrooms are supposed to be orderly. We fear the administrator or school tour or unexpected parent visit, the critical eye who will see our classrooms in such a state and know, in a moment's observation, that we have failed as teachers.

What do we do? We panic!

We direct. We redirect. We negotiate. We chide. We reprimand. We apply our homeopathic response: we fight chaos with movement. We fight fire with fire. And in doing so, we burn the whole place down.

We want our work cycles to run like peaceful water, to meander but never to crash. But consider the silent pool at the base of the waterfall. How can this violent falling emerge as such calm? Does the riverbed move to redirect the thunder of the waterfall? No. It remains still. It reminds the water through its stillness that there is no need for alarm, that peace will emerge again. It goes about its own work, stationary and supportive. What happens to the stone that protrudes through that deafening water? The water continues to crash around it, wearing it down moment by moment until it retreats behind the wall of noise. The water always wins.

Sit. Trust that the waters will calm. Model the peacefulness you know will return. If you must move, move with the river. Put your hands on the materials and work. Practice lessons you hope to show later. Focus. Concentrate. Engage. Be the path of least resistance. The water will follow.

We are here to offer to this life, which came into the world by itself, the means necessary for development, and having done that we must await this development with respect.

—*Maria Montessori*

17

The best leaders value their words, and use them sparingly.
When she has accomplished her task,
The people say, "Amazing:
We did it, all by ourselves!"

We are taught that our goal should be to be able to leave the classroom without the children noticing, to help the children to do things on their own, to give them all the tools they will need to leave us, and to do so without ever asking for credit.

Where is the joy in that? Aren't we volunteering, year after year, child after child, for the heartache of an eventual farewell? Aren't we offering, class after class, to give unconditional acceptance, irrepressible value to each child without expecting any in return? Every child we agree to love, we agree to lose. Each child we touch, we hold only long enough to let them go.

Water flows over stone. It moves past, moves on and no one notices the riverbed. But neither the water nor the rock is unaffected by this dance. The more water that passes, the smoother, the less resistant the rock becomes. The more rock over which it has flown, the richer, the more complex the water. We can see our effect on the children, even if we are not meant to speak it out loud. The water lingers around level stone, just as it races past the jagged rock.

The stone is overlooked but hardly unimportant. Who wants to look at the silent teacher when there are vibrant, joyful children to be observed? But, oh, to be the polished river rock, to have our coarse daggers replaced with cool velvet. There you can find the joy in the peaceful acceptance that your beauty emerges because of the bits of yourself you were willing to offer to the children.

And, truth be told, we *are* offered unconditional love by the children, in the same proportion as we offer it to them. How hard will even the most challenging child try to get our attention? For the dozens of children we serve each year, they will each have had only one teacher. They will hold within them, albeit sometimes unnamed, the memory of that teacher who helped them stand alone. They may not recognize you in the grocery store years later, but the water of their lives will nonetheless carry you along.

The first duty of an education is to stir up life, but leave it free to develop.

—*Maria Montessori*

18

When there is strife in the family unit,
People talk about "brotherly love."
When the country falls into chaos,
Politicians talk about "patriotism."

No school is perfect. No combination of imperfect humans muddling along their own uncharted routes will be without missteps. It is easier, sometimes, to focus on the faults of our colleagues than to pull the planks from our own eyes. We feel better about our mistakes by first acknowledging the seemingly larger ones around us. Who notices the chipped paint when the house is falling down?

How does it help, though? We critique each other. We point fingers and pick each other apart. We complain to our administrators or openly criticize each other. Do we find ourselves better heard for the hostility? Do we improve each other's practice by first tearing it down? Hardly. We know better than to ridicule the children, yet we feel totally empowered to mock each other. How would you respond to a child who surprised you with his behavior? Would you jump first to conclusions, assume you understood his motivation and intent? Or would you ask, gently, "Tell me more about that"? Would you sit beside him, observe him, try to understand how this behavior, which may seem so misguided to you, helps the child? Likewise, we can choose to gather together with our colleagues, to learn with and from them, and in turn to make them open to the support we might be able to offer.

When a single classroom is in crisis, so is the school. As members of a community, our obligation is not fulfilled when we have met the needs of the children within our own closed classrooms. Chaos spreads. When a cancer is in the body, the healthy organ cannot ignore the illness. But like the survivor who can value life because she has faced death, the learning community that brings itself through crisis so values the calm of collaboration and interreliance. It is when a classroom is in crisis that the support of the community is so dearly needed. We refortify by assuming that even those teachers with whom we disagree believe that they, too, are serving children well. We refortify by suspending disbelief, working with instead of against the other adults in our communities. Ineffective teachers, even damaging ones, are loved by the children in their care. If for no other reason than the model it offers to the children who love us, we need first to seek the redeeming and redemptive qualities in each other. We chose between building bridges or throwing stones.

That is not to say that all teachers should remain in all schools. There is a season, too, for graceful good-byes, for the recognition that competing values weaken a unified model for the children. When teachers leave, however, they need not be demonized and they need not set the house on fire simply because they didn't want to live there anymore. Offering compassionate acceptance, whatever the resolution to teaching conflicts might be, gives children a model of the graceful good-bye. There will be time in their lives when they, too, must choose to try to change their relationships or to leave them behind. When teachers leave, the full school community has the opportunity to be evidence of hope in even the most dismal human interactions—hope that even those conflicts that are insurmountable can be blessed with basic human decency, that even those quarrels we will never resolve can be left unsettled without degrading one another in the process.

If a child is to be treated differently than he is today a radical change, and one upon which everything else will depend, must first be made; and that change must be made in the adult.

—*Maria Montessori*

19

Forget about knowledge and wisdom,
And people will be a hundred times better off.
Throw away charity and righteousness,
And people will return to brotherly love.
Throw away profit and greed,
And there won't be any thieves.
Embrace simplicity.
Put others first.
Desire little.

Is every teacher infallible? Is every decision just? Does every school place children before profit? Clearly not, although in our language, in our rhetoric, we may presume. Who wants to admit that he is not wise or that she has been unethical or that he has felt greed? Particularly not teachers, who are supposed to be the conveyors of wisdom in schools, temples of integrity.

But try as we might, the daily lives of schools are usually not lofty. Administrators may want to inspire teachers through poetic calls to arms, but they are just as likely to be asked to sit with the child who has just vomited all over the language materials. Teachers may want to exude Solomon-like arbitration, but someone needs first to show the child how to blow her nose. And while we all want to avoid the issue of money, none of us wants to beg for our own dinner. Much of the lives we lead are filled up by logistics, overwhelmed by the necessaries-for-today with little time for noble pursuits. It's hard to seek the Holy Grail when you can't even find your keys.

We may not be able to change the monotony of our day-to-day responsibilities. As exalted as our rhetoric may be, which of us can be touching when we're wearing latex gloves? If we didn't claim wisdom, if we didn't pretend to be holy, perhaps we wouldn't set such a high standard for others to judge us against. If we acknowledged that our decisions are often faulty, perhaps we wouldn't be so afraid to make mistakes. And while profit may entice thieves, there is no indignity in earning a living wage.

You may not be able to drive the rhetoric from your school, your boss, or your community. But you can find a quieter place inside of it, one in which you ask of yourself what you can reasonably offer and protect for yourself that which you should reasonably protect. Holiness, justice, and money: leave them to those who seek control. It is a short fall from holy to holier than thou. It is an arm's reach from judge to executioner. Purse strings, when held improperly, cut off blood to the hands. Better to seek wisdom through experience, justice through treating each other with basic fairness, and wealth in relationships rather than ledgers.

Mothers, father, politicians: all must combine in their respect and help for this delicate work of formation, which the child carries on in the depth of a profound psychological mystery, under the tutelage of an inner guide.

—*Maria Montessori*

20

Must you fear what others fear?
Nonsense, look how far you have missed the mark!

It's the dreaded, uncomfortable conversation. Some person who has never visited our classrooms or observed our practices condemns Montessori with full confidence and vigor. "You don't really *believe* that nonsense, do you?" "Puh-lease don't give me the Montessori kids!" "Isn't that the school that teaches kids to be anarchists?" We are supposed to know how to answer these questions, but it seems so impolite to stand up to the affronts. And so instead we complain over the lunch table, where we're safely surrounded by other Montessorians, of how wrong the rest of the world is. We dig ourselves deeper into the security of our hidden dens and decide not to go to another one of "those" conferences.

Have you joined the cult? Have you drunk the Kool-Aid? Did you have the how-to-put-your-head-in-the-sand lesson? If we believe that this is first and foremost a humanitarian practice, aren't we obligated to defend it against its detractors? You have come to Montessori because it satisfied some need that was not met in traditional education. Perhaps you believe in its academic outcomes. Perhaps the peaceful communities of classrooms have convinced you. Perhaps you have observed children who do not feel the need to defend their individuality because it has been so deeply revered by their teachers. Whatever it was, there was something of a risk taker in you to have ventured down this path. Something in you sought out an alternative.

And yet, the fear remains. Will our student outcomes be high enough? Will the children get into the right elementary school, high school, college? Will we have done enough to prove Montessori works? Who are you trying to convince? Speak confidently about your values before the children arrive, and you will find yourself surrounded by the families who share those values. Speak truthfully about the child, in his glorious complexity, and trust that the school that welcomes him will be the right school. Speak knowledgeably about *why* Montessori works, and you may just inspire a convert.

To do any of these, though, requires first that we revisit the Kool-Aid. If we are to be meaningful contributors to this conversation, we must first understand the why, the how, the intricacies of Montessori beyond the specifics of our manuals. We cannot defend ourselves against detractors if we don't have any deeper understanding of Montessori than the ritualized practice of particular lessons. Montessori lessons are not justified by the steps they include. The steps they include are justified by a mindful purpose and an internalized philosophy. Every action in your classroom should stand up to examination. Every interaction should be consistent with the values you claim. It's all right that it be different, so long as it is also well thought out. When you find yourself that confident of the small choices you make as a Montessori teacher, you will be more confident of the larger defenses you may have to offer as a Montessorian.

To become acquainted with the material, a teacher should not just look at it, study it in a book, or learn its use through the explanations of another ... if a teacher has enough patience to repeat an exercise as often as a child, she can measure in herself the energy and endurance possessed by a child of a determined age. For this final purpose, the teacher can grade the materials and thus judge the capacity of a child for a certain kind of activity at a given stage of his development.

—*Maria Montessori*

21

Intangible and evasive, yet it has a manifestation.
Secluded and dark, yet there is a vitality within it.
Within it we can find order.

There is a peacefulness that is impossible to overlook in teachers who have been teaching for decades and yet still love their work. If we are like most, we remember at least one of these women or men from our own childhood. If we are lucky, we may meet one at a conference or workshop as an adult, when we are ready to learn from them in a different way. If we are exceptionally blessed, one works side by side with us every day.

From where does this peacefulness come? That ready smile, the slow movements ... nothing fazes these teachers. Surely that peace does not come from the exhaustion of a life surrounded by children! Or does it? When we begin our training, we are often overwhelmed by how much there is to do: materials to be made, paper to cut, pictures to laminate. We think that the workload will decrease as our time in the classroom grows. We hope for the day when we are finished making all the material we need. Then, years later, we are still hunched over paper cutters. We are still excited to find a new small object in an unexpected place. We still go to conference, refining our skills, asking questions, wanting to know more. The workload hasn't changed; we have just gotten used to it! We have realized that there is never a time when the materials are finished, so long as the children we serve continue to grow and change and emerge. We will never have exactly the right material at exactly the right time for every single child. But as on all wise and impossible quests, we keep moving forward. The work doesn't change.

If you see that work as a burden, as a load, it pulls at you and wears you down. Shoulders hunch. Faces frown. And over time, you find yourself more focused on the hostility you feel toward the task in front of you than on the brilliant moving dance of the children around you.

The child works diligently every day. We know that, even when he is not doing what we've told him to do, he is still at work, creating the man he is to become. There are days when this is harder work than others, days filled more with tears and frustration than joy. But the child keeps working and feels no hostility toward the task. Likewise, the work we do is helping us to create the teachers we will become. Just as the child is always growing, so are we as teachers. Just as all interactions teach the child something about the world, so do they teach us about our world, our teaching, our work. The work does not change. All that we can affect is our response to it. When we see the work of preparing the classroom as a chore, it hangs around us like a yoke. We avoid it at all costs, but the work doesn't change. When we see the work of preparing the classroom as preparing us to serve, we can find the blessing in the monotony of five-by-five-inch squares. Each material we prepare is a prayer, a tiny smiling gratitude to the children who offer us the chance to do this work well.

The teacher's skill in not interfering comes with practice, like everything else, but it never comes easily. It means rising to spiritual heights. True spirituality realizes that even to help can be a source of pride.

—*Maria Montessori*

22

Because she isn't self-centered,
People can see the light in her.
Because she does not boast of herself,
She becomes a shining example.
Because she does not glorify herself,
She becomes a person of merit.
Because she wants nothing from the world,
The world cannot overcome her.

Who are your mentors? Who are the teachers with whom you are most vulnerable, the ones to whom to confess your fears? Who is the teacher you aspire to be? Is she brash? Does he focus attention only on himself and on the successes of his classroom? Is her way always right? Do you stand in his shadow?

Or is it that teacher who listens to your question before answering it? Is it the teacher who acknowledges the challenges to her own teaching, who struggles with the rightness of his work? Is it the teacher who finds the work you've done well before suggesting alternatives? Is it the teacher whose voice is overpowering or the one with whom you feel heard?

We struggle, each of us, as teachers, against the demons of our traditional education. Teachers are supposed to be right all the time. Teachers are supposed to know the answers. Teachers are not to be questioned. But the teachers who touch our hearts, the ones whose fingerprints left seeds and not bruises on our spirits, didn't necessarily have all the answers. They shared with us a critical secret: that we were able to find them ourselves. Then they offered us the tools to begin the hunt.

When we are sharing with other teachers, which model do we become? Are we the opinionated, all-knowing, not-to-be-questioned teacher we feared as children? Our successes as teachers both of children and adults are not to be found in our ability to control them. In seeking control, in positioning ourselves to have our voices heard first and loudest, our true work falls silent. You cannot lead, no matter how tightly cinched the leash, without the willing cooperation of your follower. On the stage, the most generous actor is the one who never looks away from the speaker, the one who offers up his place in the spotlight so as not to distract the audience with its glare. Likewise, we offer more to our colleagues by serving as mirrors rather than leashes, by listening more than we speak. We offer that invaluable gift, the one we hope we will be granted ourselves but for which we can take no responsibility: a place to be heard.

The teacher, when she begins work in our schools, must have a kind of faith that the child will reveal himself through work. She must free herself from all preconceived ideas concerning the levels at which the children may be.

—*Maria Montessori*

23

If you open yourself to the Tao,
The Tao will eagerly welcome you.
If you open yourself to virtue,
Virtue will become a part of you.

Why is it that, a hundred years later, the Montessori method still works when so many other educational reforms have gone the way of the pet rock? What protects the method from cultural whims?

The answer lies in the simplicity of the method. Simple? A method that requires forty-three steps to peel a carrot is simple? Yes. At its core, before any of the materials were designed, before anyone wrote down a single lesson plan, before national organizations fought their territorial battles and schools began arguing which was a "real" Montessori school, a single element lit the wick: *Observation.*

The Montessori method continues to serve children well because it is based on that scientific observation of individual children. Conditions existed. Stimuli were presented to affect those conditions. Some preceded positive effects and were repeated over time to become part of the canon of Montessori. Each lesson you learn in training is part of that canon. Each material you purchase or prepare is part of that canon. Each sequence you memorized is part of that canon. But it is not the lesson or the material or the sequence that makes Montessori work. The lessons, the materials, that careful order of presentation, work because, and only because, they respond to the observed needs of the individual child.

But what about when they don't work? What about the child who doesn't respond the way you've expected her to? What about the child who doesn't master the material in the order you'd prefer? In the exceedingly simple model of Montessori, only one of two things could possibly have gone awry. Either you misinterpreted what you observed, or you presented a stimulus ill-designed for the task.

When we rely solely on our manuals, we build our classrooms on sand. Montessori is built first on observation, and it is only through the systemic and systematic observation of each child that you will know which material fits where. When we rely solely on our manuals, we surrender our role as scientists in the classroom. Montessori requires consistent and objective research into the conditions of each child. Montessorians often seek peace first and precision later. But it is through the specificity of unbiased observation that our compassion emerges for each child we serve. It is by understanding the needs of each child, as a unique and concrete individual, that we see his humanity.

There is a part of the child's soul that has always been unknown but which must be known. With a spirit of sacrifice and enthusiasm we must go in search, like those who travel to foreign lands and tear up mountains in their search for hidden gold.

—*Maria Montessori*

24

Those who call themselves righteous
Can't know how wrong they are.
Those who boast of their accomplishments
Diminish the things they have done.

Which of us has never made a mistake in presenting a material to a child? Which of us has never loved a material in which the children showed no interest? Our hearts, so deeply invested in the miniature objects we've collected, cry out when they are not equally important to the children. We fault the child for not paying close enough attention while our presentations are falling apart. We send the child out of circle for wiggling instead of watching.

Every interaction teaches the child about his world, about her relationship with learning, with school, and with us. Every time we commend a child for valuing what we value or condemn a child for her lack of interest, we ask the child to be more like us, to love what we love and want what we want. We present the materials we love the best and smile when the children show equal interest. We tell the children that we want them to view us as their guides, and then we reprimand them when they have not followed step by step in our footprints.

Let go.

The work that lasts is not found in the materials on the shelf. It is in the strength of the relationships you have built with the children in your care. It is in the respect that you show for their path, wherever it may lead, and the knowledge you may offer in tools for the discoveries ahead. We carry a dual obligation: to follow the child and to prepare him for life. We must be both responsive and responsible. Would you have done your work as a Montessorian if you had never given the child the specific tools she would need to survive as a student, if you had never introduced her to reading, to

47

math, to geography? Would you have done your work as a Montessorian if that was *all* that motivated you, if every choice was justified by whether the child's academic growth was propelled? We need to be both. We offer both by understanding the purpose of the materials and by observing the child intently to know when the time is right to introduce them. But a classroom filled with beautiful materials is not a Montessori classroom. The classroom becomes a Montessori classroom when the teacher's preparation of that specially designed environment is with individual children in mind. Put aside the pride you need for that new material and take your satisfaction instead in finding the material that met the children's needs.

The child is much more spiritually elevated than is usually supposed. He often suffers, not from too much work, but from work that is unworthy of him.

—*Maria Montessori*

25

Humanity follows the Earth.
Earth follows Heaven.
Heaven follows the Tao.
The Tao follows only itself.

Here are the Great Lessons, the massive time lines of life and development, the materials designed in their enormity to give some concrete sense of how very small we are. We wait, though, until our children are older, to show them the interaction of the earth and her sisters, to unroll that endless black cord. We wait until they can think abstractly, as though our place in the universe were an abstraction.

The Great Lessons—they are the great questions, the ones we are driven to understand from before we are born. The whats and whys of our existence. When are we too young to ask? When are we too old?

Younger children ask these same questions, although their language may not be as complex. Babies in the Nido cry in sympathy to each other. Children rush around the friend who has fallen from the swings. Our daughters, our sons comfort us when we can't find the words to describe our sadness. In younger children who have not yet been taught about hierarchies, the idea of unified, interreliant life is concrete. When we plant a button it does not grow. When we plant a seed it does. Man makes some things, but some things are made with such singular wonder that humans can only watch them blossom. For younger children, these are opportunities for wonder, not fear.

We have taught children to feel separate from one another. "Don't worry about him." "Go back to work." "She doesn't need your help." And so, eventually, the idea of that interreliance must be presented again as a new lesson, a new concept to be mastered. Because we struggle with our

49

responsibility to each other as adults, we create that same struggle in the children we teach.

Separate. The earth will still spin. Accept. The earth will still spin. Children are born understanding. Children are born, understanding.

The needs of mankind are universal. Our means of meeting them create the richness and diversity of the planet. The Montessori child should come to relish the texture of that diversity.

—Maria Montessori

26

If you abandon yourself to foolishness,
You lose touch with your beginnings.
If you let yourself become distracted,
You will lose the basis of your power.

Do you remember your training? The enthusiasm you found in mastering a material with which you had struggled, or finally understanding why a box of prisms worked together the way it did....We forget about the joys we found when we discovered Montessori. We felt like rebels, like valiant explorers uncovering a hidden oasis. We were motivated by the newness, the unearthing, the mystery.

But not all things are mysterious. Like marriages, teachers mature with Montessori. They get comfortable. They stop trying to impress. They forget to kiss good night. We lose our enthusiasm for the classroom. It becomes a place we know so well that we don't have to think about it anymore. And in so becoming, it becomes a place we value less for the familiarity.

So, like a businessman with a seven-year itch, we go to conferences. We see some new material or alternative reading system. We see a computer program to teach math. It's shiny. It's new. Surely it will work better, faster than the old standby Montessori materials. We find space on the shelves. We move other materials out of the way.

Sometimes, they stick around. Sometimes, that new material really does fill a need that had been gaping in our classrooms. But most of the time, they lose their luster. They don't work as well as we thought they might. They become clutter in the storage rooms, too new to discard but not quite useful enough to display.

Our teaching is a fundamentally human endeavor. We teach differently in Montessori because of what we believe to be those core human values, the tendencies of man. The nudge we need sometimes, the second honey-moon, is better found in the humanity we share with other teachers than in the materials we can stuff into our luggage. Talk to other teachers. Break bread. Laugh together. Scrub shelves together. Montessori, a constant companion, can nonetheless leave us feeling very lonely. Find companionship and laughter and renewal in the mix.

To keep alive that enthusiasm is the secret of real guidance, and it will not provide a difficult task, provided that the attitude towards the child's acts be that of respect, calm, and waiting, and provided that he be left free in his movements and experiences.

—Maria Montessori

27

What is a good person but a bad person's teacher?
What is a bad person but raw material for his teacher?
If you fail to honor your teacher or fail to enjoy your student,
You will become deluded no matter how smart you are.

Throughout history, throughout religious narratives, is the story of knowledge and judgment. When we learn to judge, we separate ourselves. When we learn to judge, we are thrown out of the garden.

"Good children" implies that some children are "bad." Most of us would shudder to hear a teacher tell a child she was bad. At what age does that become appropriate? At what age does the child become the bad man, bad woman, bad teacher? At what age is it too late to show compassion?

Compassion—from the Latin *com* and *pate*: to suffer together. Compassion requires us to acknowledge the suffering in others, not to judge or criticize but to recognize that at some point along the way this other *became* other. This person came to see himself as we will now so gladly label him: bad, good, deficient, enough. Which of us has not wondered the same about ourselves? Which of us has not suffered worrying whether we are good *enough*, successful *enough*, kind *enough*, giving *enough*? Which of us has not sat lonely in our otherness?

In these times, when our children are increasingly violent, when hurting each other seems to come so much more easily, we are trapped in that otherness. Children do not spontaneously kill. But it is so much simpler to call the children who are hurt "senseless victims" and the children who pull triggers "evil" than to suffer together with them all. We want to think of ourselves as never capable of atrocity. We want to push away our culpability, but our hearts ache when we hear of another child, gunned down in a school. We suffer together.

The child is the spiritual builder of mankind, and obstacles to his free development are the stones in the wall by which the soul of man has become imprisoned.

—*Maria Montessori*

28

Know the masculine,
But keep to the feminine:
And become a watershed to the world.
If you embrace the world,
The Tao will never leave you
And you become as a little child.

Where is the creativity in Montessori? Where is the imagination in a method that values one presentation, one sequence, one position of the hand? Don't we sacrifice our children's inventiveness by giving them only self-correcting materials?

Keep to the female: from receptivity emerges creativity. When we offer children the world, as it really exists and in endless quantity, we build in them that receptivity. There is always more to learn. There is always another question to ask.

Curiosity is an empty space, a question to be answered. When children have had this curiosity filled, they can be truly creative.

Think of the great works of art, the pieces of literature that have moved you or the music within which you have gladly been lost. What makes great art? Clearly there is no prescription. Great art speaks universally because it reflects the universal experience, an experience that can only be understood by living it. Children do not build their imaginations by escaping into fantastic diversions. Children build their imaginations by experiencing imagination. In imagining children living around the world, children put into those conceptions bits of what they understand from their own. They may never have tasted a particular spice, but they know what bitter tastes like, and so they imagine. They may never visit the Eiffel Tower, but they know how far back their necks have to reach to look up at the highest buildings in their towns, and so they imagine. They may not fully understand the suffering of a child who has been orphaned by war, but they know what it feels like to miss their parents, and so they imagine. From these imaginings, their creativity is born. Not mimicking representations of the cartoon character they've studied on a lunch box, but true creativity: the turn of phrase that somehow captures a complicated thought, the mix of color that conveys intense emotion, the fluidity of music that speaks sadness or joy. Creativity blossoms from truth received.

Education is a natural process carried out by the human individual, and is acquired not by listening to words, but by experiences in the environment.

—Maria Montessori

29

Do you want to rule the world and control it?
I don't think it can ever be done.
The world is a sacred vessel
And it cannot be controlled.
You will only make it worse if you try.

Where is the worth in a movement that seeks to change the interactions of adults if the world cannot be improved? Is all our work for naught?

The world is sacred. As Montessori teachers, it is easy to focus on the problems. Our energies are better focused on the solutions in front of us. If the children kept bumping into a shelf, would you blame the child or move the shelf? Likewise, when a conflict appears in the life of the child, do we blame the child or do we look for the obstacle we have created?

We distance ourselves from the people we see as the problem. We blame parents, and in so doing send messages to the child that her family is lacking. We blame each other, and in so doing ask the child to choose which teacher to believe. We don't get to choose which lessons the child absorbs—every experience the child has teaches him something. But we can choose whether or not we acknowledge that those yearning, seeking minds are paying attention. We can choose whether we objectify children by asking them to do as we say and not as we do, or whether we acknowledge their perfection by putting aside our own pride. The natural lives of children emerge as they are meant to emerge. We get in the way, plant competitiveness, plant control, plant judgment, and then blame the child for the harvest.

Trust that the world, in the life of each child, starts anew, sacred. The inherent wisdom of children can be trusted, just as you can place bets that an adult has planted the behavior that annoys you. Understand that if we are to change the harvest, it comes from the seeds we plant and not from condemning the fertile and sacred soil of the child.

> *No social problem is as universal as the oppression of the child.*
> *—Maria Montessori*

30

Those who lead people by following the Tao
Don't use weapons to enforce their will.
Using force always leads to unseen troubles.

We're pretty sure we have figured out how to treat children, but how effective have we been in treating adults? School administrators rely on punishments and power, then are surprised when teachers look for other schools. Teachers talk at parents, then are surprised that they lack involvement and support from their families.

For every force there is a counterforce. Adults no more want to be controlled than children do, and yet we find ourselves building more and more complicated hierarchies in our schools. We pretend that they are still consistent with our Montessori philosophy. We call them "coordinators" instead of "supervisors." We "facilitate" instead of "direct."

Language is important, but when the language we choose is not reflected in the actions we take, language becomes a violent hypocrisy. We cannot hide behind our carefully chosen phrases. Even if we call them communities, we cannot run our schools like armies. There are no generals in Montessori.

As administrators and teacher educators, we ask teachers to abdicate control of their classrooms to the children, then we hold out rewards and punishments to teachers' behavior. Montessori teachers support the society by cohesion by helping the children to rely on each other. Montessori administrators so often undermine that same society in their faculty, by micromanaging every teacher action. Yes, schools need continuity. They need systems and principles upon which everyone can rely. But those principles can either be forced down by heavy-handed administrators or they can be built by the collaboration of individuals throughout the school community. Principles can either be articulated standards, universally applied throughout a program, or they can be shallow brochure slogans distant from the real lives of schools. When principles count, they are applied as consistently to the administrators as they are to the teachers.

We rely on the teacher to prepare the environment. Likewise, if there is to be change in the adult communities of schools, it is to come from the administrator. We rely on the teacher to put aside her ego and pride, to support a classroom within which children are working as though she didn't exist. Likewise, as administrators we must be willing to surrender our control, to build up instead of forcing down. We must be willing, as administrators, to build the trust with our faculty that precedes community and to measure ourselves by the same yardstick as we measure our teachers. Leadership is modeling, not militant.

The prize and punishment are incentives toward unnatural or forced effort, and therefore we cannot speak of the natural development of the child in connection with them.

—*Maria Montessori*

31

Weapons are meant for destruction,
And thus are avoided by the wise.
Only as a last resort
Will a wise person use a deadly weapon.
If peace is her true objective,
How can she rejoice in the victory of war?

Violence surrounds us. Children see people hurting each other throughout their lives, from the hyperviolent images hidden behind the veil of animation to strangers yelling at each other in traffic. As Montessorians, we abhor the intense violence that seems to pervade our society. We say that our practice is humanitarian, that children will be secure in a peaceful planet if we preserve their peacefulness through education.

But violence is often quiet, and weapons sly. We redirect the child who has hurt another, but we may overlook the myriad of other means of force that the child silently endures. If our efforts are only focused on the vulgar dramatic displays, we teach that cunning violence is acceptable. Just don't get caught.

What are the quiet weapons? Physical force: the idea that being taller or older or stronger gives us the right to inflict our will on the child. The force of our voices: that being louder, firmer, angrier gives us the right to demand the child's attention. When we raise our voices at children, our weapons are no less hurtful. The lessons are far more dangerous.

Vulgar displays are concrete. We can make them black-and-white. Do not hit. Do not bite. But it is much harder to define the subtler weapons, except through the guilt they leave in us as teachers. We may hide our remorse behind justifications of how the child caused our reaction. We may commiserate with other adults about that kid who drives us all crazy. In defending ourselves, we draw clearly our hypocrisy. We may not want to say out loud that we have mistreated the child. But in our quieter hearts, we know it when we feel it.

That is not to say that the impulses of the child are never to be countered. Of course, you will hold the child who wants to dash into the busy street. You might even hold the child whose anger is so intense that she can no longer express it with the limited language of childhood. In these moments, though, we draw the line between violence and protection by the compassion that we bring to the child. If you pulled your spouse back from the path of a speeding car, would your first response be to hold him or to berate him? Would you respond from the fear of seeing the person you so loved in danger or from the frustration of the disruption his oversight caused to your walk? When force is necessary, let it be compassionate action.

A new education from birth onwards must be built up. Education must be reconstructed and based on the law of nature and not on the preconceived notions and prejudices of adult society.

—Maria Montessori

32

The Tao is nameless and unchanging,
Although it appears insignificant,
Nothing in the world can contain it.

How complicated are the children, really? We can track their development, predict emerging skills, judge their growth spurts, chart their progress. Doesn't it all look pretty much the same in the end? Children come to us, they learn with us, they move on. Three-year-olds become four-year-olds. Four-year-olds become five-year-olds. And so on. And on. And on.

Over time, over children, we grow more comfortable in what to expect, and so can better understand the child whose development is surprising. But in that comfort, we can sometimes project on to children what we expect of their development, when we should be responding to it because we have seen it concretely in each child. Don't the children all become wild in the spring? Isn't December always a difficult month? Doesn't the best work of the year happen in January and February? Perhaps. Maybe not.

Remember the secret of childhood? What is the secret? That inner drive, that push that we cannot perceive, that we can no longer understand because we are no longer children. In our loss of words, we seek other ways to demystify children. We track and predict and judge and chart. We put children's development onto clearly defined, carefully laid-out spreadsheets for their parents to understand. We justify. Checklists are easier for teachers to complete. They are easier for parents to understand. But what about the details that don't fit into the boxes? We overlook the unique wonderment of each child by focusing instead on the predictors that we have chosen. We come up with our list of the individual traits that we value, and we check off when the child has shown them, and so abdicate our duty to continue to try to perceive the uncountable galaxies within each child.

If we are unable to easily give details, if it is too difficult or time-consuming to describe the unique wonderment of each child, we are not paying close enough attention. Montessori is based on the attention to each individual. Children come before our manuals. We should know, at any moment, the endless ways in which two children are different, or we are not watching carefully enough. Using a checklist for its simplicity has its merits. But don't pretend that children are simple. Leave space for the unexpected, and know that every child is unexpected.

The secret of good teaching is to regard the child's intelligence as a fertile field in which seeds may be sown, to grow under the heat of flaming imagination.

—*Maria Montessori*

33

Those who know others are intelligent;
Those who know themselves are truly wise.
Those who master others are strong;
Those who master themselves have true power.

Montessori requires frequent, regular looking outward. We are trained to observe others, to make determinations based on what we have seen. And so this becomes habitual. We forget to turn the focus to ourselves.

We feel more comfortable when we know where we are. We find confidence in our navigation. Isn't this one of our great tendencies? To orient ourselves? Our point of view blinds.

The danger of this outlooking is that it leaves little space for our own accountability. We give lip service to removing the obstacles that we create, but how do we know what they are if we haven't attended to ourselves?

Find the time for innerlooking. Journaling is one way. Some of us keep journals that we use to help document our classrooms, but any writing describes its author more acutely than its subject. Use your journal to document yourself. Have you ever found an old diary, one from your childhood or your adolescence? Remember that feeling of being an observer to the person you once were. Your journals from yesterday are the same, if the changes more subtle. Time gives distance to all things, even to ourselves.

When we have developed the means to look inward, to distance ourselves from the daily pounding of our current values and priorities, we gain the ability to look forward, to judge how who we are today relates to who we hope to be, as teachers and as travelers in this human endeavor.

When we have developed the means to look inward, we see our hand in the obstacles around us, in the ones we set up for the children and the ones we set up for ourselves. We find our accountability and in so doing can begin the work of changing the effects of our hands. In so doing, we can begin the work of changing the paths of our lives.

The training of the teacher is something far more than learning ideas. It includes the training of character. It is a preparation of the spirit.

—*Maria Montessori*

34

It nourishes infinite worlds,
Yet it doesn't seek to master the smallest creature.
Because it does not seek greatness,
It is able to accomplish truly great things.

Stuff stuff stuff. Paper paper paper. When did our Montessori process become about product? When did the photocopier become the most useful tool in our schools?

But there is so much to do, and parents want paper. We must send things home. We must prove ourselves. How much does a piece of construction paper tell a parent about his child? How much does a handout inform, even if all the answers are correct? We know these tokens are not important to the child, who will toil endlessly on a piece of handiwork only to forget later that it is his. We persist in them because they provide us some confidence, some time, some means to communicate something, anything, to each other.

We often think of paper as proof. It is evidence of what we are teaching or of how well the children learn. Imagine the child multiplying with golden beads or factoring on the Peg-Board or building complicated sentences with the moveable alphabet. Does that eight-by-eleven sheet really capture the work the child invested? Have we documented the child's work or illustrated some lesser skill?

Paper goes out. People come in. If you want to prove to parents how much their children are learning, invite them to join your classroom for a morning. Find time. Make time. Why do only parents attend back-to-school nights? How can you describe a Montessori classroom without children in it? If we are to value the processes of the children's work, we have to find ways to emphasize those processes. The parent who understands her child's Montessori experience does not need the paper.

This challenge falls to us. We can take the simpler answer, photocopy another handout, precut some more circles for snowmen glued on blue paper. Or when the children need more challenging work, we can prepare more challenging work. We can teach the children to fill their time copying and mimicking our products or we can teach them to pursue their own processes. It is not the child's responsibility to prove that he has learned something. That is a private duty we hold with parents. When we force the child to create extrinsic products, we distance him from his intrinsic motivation. When we allow this to be the way we prove ourselves to parents, we compromise our values as Montessorians in exchange for the ease of the green button on the machine.

But in those countries where the toy-making industry is less advanced, you will find children with quite different tastes. They are also calmer, more sensitive and happy. Their one idea is to take part in the activities going on about them.

—Maria Montessori

35

She who follows the way of the Tao
Will draw the world to her steps.
She can go without fear of being injured,
Because she has found peace and tranquility in her heart.

Montessori doesn't always go right. There are times when our limits as adults, or the limits of our resources as schools, cannot answer the child's need. A child whose behavior challenges, who does not respond in the ways we have come to predict forces us to change our expectations. Is the adult able to offer more? Is the child? Sometimes the answer is no.

What are the steps we take in these times, when our commitment to Montessori is shaken? Do we judge the child and condemn him? Do we throw up our hands in exasperation? Blame parents? Diagnose?

First, we look to ourselves and to the obstacles we may have unwittingly created. We ask for help from our colleagues. We get other sets of eyes, other scientists and servants and saints to observe. We may ask parents what works at home or what is not working. Sometimes we find the answer. Sometimes we don't.

We can see these situations in terms of children who do not "fit" Montessori, or we can see them as further evidence of the extraordinary complexity of each child. Because Montessori is child-centered, there is no child to whom it cannot respond. But schools are not infinite pools of financial resources any more so than adults are infinite pools of emotional ones. Very often we find the answer. Very often we don't.

We still have the same duties of loyalty, of service to the child whom we can't serve as to the children we can. Keeping a child enrolled whose needs cannot be met by this particular school is no service to the child. Keeping parents in the dark when we have come to the bottom of our professional bags of tricks is no service to the child. We are not being nice. We are being proud. We are not being compassionate. We are being cowardly. Difficult conversations are necessary. Difficult conversations about one's child are excruciatingly painful. And necessary. Let those conversations come from a recognition that the limits are ours, that it is our reserve and not the child's potential that is lacking. Let them be firmly seated in the humility of our lacking. Sometimes we serve the child best by acknowledging that we cannot serve him well.

The adult must find within himself the still unknown error that prevents him from seeing the child as he is.

—*Maria Montessori*

36

If you want something to be removed,
You must first allow it to flourish.
If you want to possess something,
You must first give it away.
This is called the subtle understanding
Of how things are meant to be.

We all have defects as teachers. Sometimes they are academic. We may not understand or feel competent with an area of the curriculum, and so we ignore it. Sometimes they are personal. We may not particularly like a parent (or his child), and so we let the other teachers interact with him. Sometimes they are spiritual, physical, emotional. There are myriad ways in which we could be more effective in our work, more peaceful in our lives, more loving or compassionate. But mostly, we ignore them.

It is very difficult, sometimes insurmountably so, to face our weaknesses. Think, though, about the teacher who prefers math and language to practical life. If she avoids presenting those lessons, what will happen to the math materials? What will happen to language? When we avoid acknowledging the things we would prefer to discard, their effect becomes magnified, not decreased. The untended wound infects.

Say it aloud: I am not perfect. Say it aloud and often and with an audience. Tell the children. Ask their help. Tell your colleagues. Ask their help. Say it aloud and guess what? It turns out you weren't hiding it very well anyway! Everyone else already knew! What brings us to improving ourselves, when we have been taught by our culture that we are as adults supposed to be finished already, is admitting to ourselves that we're not finished. When we hide behind the façade of completion, we forget that the walls we've built are invisible. Others can still see you inside. They're just less able to touch you. You have been the audience to other people's walls. You have known teachers who were so competent that you didn't feel you had anything to offer and so didn't offer anything.

Discard the emperor's new clothes. By acknowledging the ways in which we are naked, the ways in which we are vulnerable, we might find warmth.

In their dealings with children adults do not become egotistic but egocentric. They look upon everything pertaining to a child's soul from their own point of view and, consequently, their misapprehensions increase.

—*Maria Montessori*

37

If rulers could follow the way of the Tao,
Then all creation would willingly follow their example.

Who are the real decision makers? Are they the teachers? The parents? The administrators? Local boards of education? National policy makers? Who affects most deeply the lives of the children in your classroom?

As Montessorians, we trust that the children whom we have served will help to improve the world when they are adults. This is no short-term process! One generation of children touches another. One small group of children grows to affect a larger group. But we are many lifetimes away from the tipping point. We know that but for the limits of the adult, the child's promise can be met. We know that but for the limits of the adult, the world could be at peace. Hopes and dreams in the cacophony of a violent world.

In the meantime, what? Who are the decision makers? We are asked to sacrifice parts of Montessori, but who is to say which parts of the method are essential and which can be discarded? In bureaucracy, others decide. In practice, we do. We determine whether or not to have faith in this method. We determine whether or not to accept it fully or to impose our separate assessments.

Montessori is a spiritual venture and like all others requires the willing suspension of disbelief. What if it doesn't work? What if this whole humanitarian exercise is somehow fundamentally flawed? What if it will never work? Has it yet? In a hundred years, have we yet changed the world? To paraphrase Narnia's Puddleglum, wouldn't you rather live in a world in which it *could* happen than in one that leaves no room for hope?

We will be given mandates, ones that we cannot choose to ignore. But within even the most restrictive commandments there is room for simple faith.

Not in the service of any political or social creed should the teacher work, but in the service of the complete human being, able to exercise in freedom a self-disciplined will and judgment, unperverted by prejudice and undistorted by fear.

—Maria Montessori

38

The Master does not force virtue on others,
Thus she is able to accomplish her task.
The ordinary person who uses force
Will find that they accomplish nothing.

You can tell a true Montessorian by how long it takes to find her in the classroom. The ones who question Montessori are easy to identify. They're loud. They're central. They draw attention. The ones who believe are hidden among the children, on the floor, behind a shelf, busy working with instead of lording over their classrooms.

Montessorians lead by example, not by noise. They know their messages are better heard when offered quietly. They remember their role. Neither the scientist, the servant, nor the saint seeks the spotlight. One observes. One prepares. One surrenders. The scientist gains recognition by observing something unique in his practice. The servant gains appreciation by silently satisfying needs. The saint gains admiration by the life she has led, not the control she has assumed. Wise Montessorians know that the value of their work will be found in the children they have served, not in the attention they have called to themselves.

A humbling practice, indeed. Who is the servant to us? Even the fastest flowing river depends on rain. Without something to replenish us, our teaching and our spirits dry out. We must find ways to refresh one another, to recognize when one of us has so given outward that our reserves are running dry. Some of this work can and should fall to our administrators. Strong administrators attend to their teachers' needs in the same way that they ask the teachers to serve their children. But just as we share different secrets with friends than with our parents, we need one another's camaraderie. We need the friendship of our peers.

There is so much else to do, and the nature of Montessori is to think first of the children. When we make time for our own spirits to be replenished, though, we give ourselves the stamina to better serve the children. Dry blood flows slowly. Find the time for companionship, even if it is while you together serve the children. You can help another teacher clean her classroom in half the time it would take to do it alone. You can prepare materials more quickly with four hands than two. In a practice that so often leaves us silent, find the space for the joyful noise and share the music with one another.

It is necessary for the teacher to guide the child without letting him feel her presence too much, so that she may always be ready to supply the desired help, but may never be the obstacle between the child and his experience.

—*Maria Montessori*

39

The great view the small as their source,
And the high takes the low as their foundation.
Their greatest asset becomes their humility.

In the course of three short years, we help the child to emerge from a toddling little life with slurred words and short steps to the confident leader. From barely being able to lift a jug unassisted to performing four-digit operations with the golden beads. From being able to hear only the most distinct differences in cylinders of sand to writing and reading at length.

In the elementary classroom, the before-and-after is even more distinct!

Our academics are so strong. Parents gape at the ease with which their children perform such challenging tasks. Our math materials excel. Small children understand factors and fractions, using words like "multiplicand" and "quotient."

It's easy to overlook the materials that do not explicitly build a child's academic skills. It's easy to emphasize the sandpaper letters instead of walking the ellipse or to reserve the math materials for the lead teacher and the cultural materials for the assistant.

We need not sacrifice one for the other, though. The math materials are more fascinating when we understand their presence all around us. The language materials are only useful if there is a world worth talking about. When we emphasize the cultural materials, we provide the child with a gift he may find only in Montessori. All life begins together. The purpose, the mathematics and poetry of this universe are evident, if we'll only look. Aren't we learning to measure and compare when we lay out life cycles? Aren't we learning language when we locate mountain ranges on the maps? Yes, and so much more. In our mathematic pursuits, we glimpse the intricate web of interdependence in our universe. In our language pursuits, we give voice to the unspeakable wonder of life.

Which are the more valuable lessons? We need not choose. When we do, it is like we have chosen which part of the puzzle can represent it all. It's only by starting with the big picture on the box that we know how the pieces fit together.

There are many who hold, as I do, that the most important part of life is not the age of university studies, but the first one, the period from birth to the age of six. For that is the time when a man's intelligence itself, his greatest implement, is being formed. But not only his intelligence; the full totality of his psychic powers.

—Maria Montessori

40

All movement returns to the Tao.

Every year, we begin again. Every year, we wonder how in the world we had the stamina to survive the year before. There is a grace in short memories. If we remembered how difficult the beginning of each cycle is, we might not have the courage to begin again.

Each year we struggle. Our classrooms begin in such chaos. Children are crying. Mothers are crying. Fathers are crying. When everyone's gone home, we are crying! Pitchers of water crash in the kitchen. Golden beads hide in the cabinet out of fear. Toes are stubbed on unattended chairs. The toilets overflow.

We are birthing our classrooms again and find ourselves in the sweaty, wet redness of hard labor. Like mothers with many children, it doesn't get easier, but we gain perspective. We trust that the children and the classroom will calm. We know that the fear will subside.

There is a gift for each of us in this cycle. Each autumn brings us rebirth. Each school year gives us the chance to begin again, to apply the lessons we learned from our mistakes. Each school year gives us the chance to be young again, even on the days when we feel like we may be too old for this!

There is danger, too. Each year, we agree again to love the children we will lose in ten months. Each year, we agree to the briefest moment's glimpse of the peace it creates before it is time again to say good-bye. Amazingly, our vulnerable hearts keep beating. We return again and again.

Cycles do what cycles do. They build, rise, crest, and begin again.

That is the nature of schools. Love dearly each beginning. Mourn dearly each good-bye. Begin again.

The child passes little by little from the unconscious to the conscious, treading always in the paths of joy and love.

—*Maria Montessori*

41

The level path seems rough,
The superior path seems empty.
The Tao hides in the unnamed
Yet it alone nourishes and completes all things.

At its core, the Montessori method is a fairly simple structure. Follow the child. Prepare the environment. Simple to complex. Concrete to abstract. Logical, simple, unsophisticated.

It takes knowledge of the complex to know how to simplify it. It takes knowledge of the abstract to identify the concrete. Do we walk away from our teacher-education programs understanding the complexity? Should we?

For many of us, the intricacies of Montessori are too much to digest in the short time we have to complete our training. We hold tight to our manuals, hoping that in the regular reperformance of these rituals, we will come to understand their mystical purpose. We repeat lessons in the precise sequence we have been taught, sneaking time with the hope that practice will shed light on the shadows.

OK, then. Hold fast. Like the man overboard, cling to whatever accepts your grasp if it keeps you afloat. But don't lose sight of the ship. You may be able to keep your head above water, but you'll be lost in the wake if you don't keep moving forward.

Read more. Learn more. Reread the original texts and reread them again. Own your knowledge by uncovering it at its source instead of relying on the rumors and stories of other explorers.

If you don't continue to learn beyond the certificate hanging on your wall, you will have only the voices of your teachers to guide you. Montessori teaching takes reflection, time to process, and life passing in practice. If you have never questioned your training, you will not know which new voices to trust. When you seek advice, you need first to know not only what you believe but why. Your learning, too, will go from simple to complex, from concrete to abstract. Your manuals are simple. Your manuals are concrete. Eventually, you must move past them into real understanding of how Montessori works, of why Montessori works.

Without that understanding, we are treading water.

The first thing required of a teacher is that he be rightly disposed for his task.

—Maria Montessori

42

People despise being orphaned, widowed, and poor.
But the noble ones take these as their titles.
In losing, much is gained.
And in gaining, much is lost.

Montessori is a lonely practice, even for the teacher surrounded by good friends. In each moment, we are self-questioning. In each moment, we are asked to surrender ourselves for the sake of the child. What of us is left?

There are so many children in the classroom but often only a single teacher. The more education we have, the more distinct we are even from the other adults in the classroom. Even when we share the space of our classrooms, we are alone.

There is life in this solitude, like the transcendental life of prayer. By embracing our unique role in the classroom, by seeking more dearly the shadow of the child in which to hide ourselves, we are connected to the tens of thousands of Montessori pilgrims in their own classrooms throughout the world. We may be isolated, but we are working together toward a different world that will spread far beyond the walls of our classroom.

The great painter signs her name inconspicuously, so as not to detract from the subject of her work. But brushstrokes are still there. Even the unsigned masterpiece betrays the name of its creator.

Likewise, our children are our great work, our brushstrokes visible long past when they have left us. The art is not about us, but it reveals us still. Our goal is not the colored canvas but the emotion it evokes when we have long since put down our brushes.

This teaching is a lonely practice. Our communion is found in our art.

The first aim of the prepared environment is, as far as it is possible, to render the growing child independent of the adult.

—Maria Montessori

43

Few in the world can comprehend
The teaching without words
Or understand the value of nonaction.

Montessori? Isn't that the place where the kids aren't allowed to speak? Can't you tell how "good" a Montessori classroom is by how quiet it is?

Wise Montessori teachers let the materials speak for themselves, but they don't seek to silence children. Our quiet is not intended to restrict but to release. When we have hushed our own voices, we can better hear the voices of the children.

Hush now. Quiet down. Advice better given to ourselves than the children. Our noisy exclamations are one more way to bring ourselves back to the center of attention. We are abrupt, shocking, in charge. We should no more yell at a child to be quiet than we should shake him in order to keep still.

Remember the three types of sound: noise, music, and the human voice. Montessori classrooms make noise, although wise Montessori teachers rarely do. Classrooms clang. Glass tinkles against glass. Chairs scrape on wood. Boxes slam. Noise, noise, noise!

The children, not hearing us, can attend to our other examples. Not hearing us, the children's other senses get involved. They watch more carefully. They taste more acutely. They touch more sensitively. Not hearing our voices, the children listen in other ways. Over time, other sounds take over. Bells chime. Music boxes tingle. Children's voices rise joyfully. When we refrain from adding to the noise, we allow space for music and voice.

We trust the children to mirror us. When we are noisy, they are noisy. When we are quiet, they are quiet. But silent rapture is not the same as silence. Be careful that, in removing your own voice, you are not asking the same of the child. Use your silence to focus attention, but do not make silence the goal. If we are to value pure silence, we must be willing to give up music. If we are to value pure silence, we refuse to hear the voice of the child.

But all of a sudden, he wakes up and hears delicious music; all his fibers begin to vibrate. The baby might think that no other sound had ever reached his ears, but really it was because his soul was not responsive to other sounds. Only human speech had any power to stir him.

—Maria Montessori

44

Which is more valuable, your possessions or your person?
Which is more destructive, success or failure?

Who are your happy converts? Perhaps you have convinced the parents of children in your classroom. Perhaps you have finally found the way to answer the questions posed to you by strangers. Perhaps it is only in your own beliefs about teaching and children that new light has been shed.

As Montessorians, we have a long history of isolation. We stand apart from other educators. We expect them to come to us if they want to know about our practice. We speak with implicit disdain about "traditional schools." We criticize other "so-called Montessori" schools.

Sometimes, it seems that we are more concerned with keeping control of the name of Montessori than we are with getting this to as many children as we can. Does it matter what we call this practice or does it matter that we serve children?

What would happen if we put aside our terms-of-art and saw ourselves instead as missionaries to a cause? What would happen if we saw our purpose as spreading the word instead of stealing the spotlight? Wasn't there a time when you didn't know as much about Montessori as you know now? Should you have been ignored, disdained, or disparaged?

We need not sacrifice the ideals of Montessori in sharing the lessons we've learned. Indeed, in holding so tightly to our own definitions of what Montessori is and isn't, we limit it to only the small window of possibility we can imagine. Have you learned all there is to know about children? Have you learned all there is to know about teaching? Are you all finished now? Isn't it possible that by opening ourselves to dialogue about Montessori, we may even improve this practice? Isn't it possible that by sharing ourselves more generously, we may find ourselves again students instead of teachers? Sometimes it seems easier to hide what we believe when we fear it might be questioned. We must be willing to hear the questions.

High in our glass schoolhouses, we still dare to throw stones.

A man is not what he is because of the teachers he has had, but because of what he has done.

—Maria Montessori

45

Movement overcomes the cold,
And stillness overcomes the heat.
That which is pure and still is the universal ideal.

You have observed the child. You have practiced the presentation. You offer it. She refuses. Or worse yet, she follows you, yawns, looks away, puts the material back on the shelf again when you have stepped away. Whose fault is it?

Is it the child's? She didn't ask for the presentation. She may even have been compliant enough to humor you while you finished.

Is it yours? You observed the child. You had reason to think it was the right material, the right day, the right moment.

Abandon fault. Leave behind the blame placing. Even the best teaching is messy.

There is so much more than we can observe. To think otherwise is to say that the child is completely open to us at all times. To think otherwise is to oversimplify the life of the child. We can observe. We can plan and prepare. And it still might not go the way we'd hoped.

Step out of the way. The child's development will continue to unfold. There is no shame in having mispredicted the response of a child. There is useful humility in recognizing that there is far more about the child than you can perceive. There is far more going on in the child's mind, in her family, in her spirit and life than your myopic eyes will ever see. Be grateful for the missteps, because they remind us that this practice is not about predictability but about embracing the complexity of each individual life we serve. When we fall short as teachers, we are that much more aware of how high our goals really are. Keep climbing.

We must help the child act, think, and will for himself. This is the art of serving the spirit, an art which can be practiced to perfection only when working with children.

—Maria Montessori

46

When the world follows the Tao,
Horses run free to fertilize the fields.
When the world does not follow the Tao,
Warhorses are bred outside the cities.

What are our countries? The real space over which we are territorial, around which we draw boundaries and borders? Our schools, our trainings, our national Montessori organizations? We take great pride in announcing our training affiliations or in disparaging the quality of another's. We discuss whose training is "real" Montessori and who is in it for the money (as though there were any money in Montessori!). The pride we insulate ourselves with is divisive. It draws attention to the many differences instead of focusing on the elements of Montessori we share in common.

Does the structure of the course matter if the students are well served? We can ask this question of classrooms at all levels of development, from infancy through adulthood. If we believe that all learners are unique, at what point do we expect them to all benefit from the same kind of program? Perhaps one teacher will be best served by a six-week intensive and another by learning across two years. What is most important is that the learning needs of the students, even as adults, have been met. Because there is no single model of learning style (a belief we share as Montessorians), to suggest that there is a single model for Montessori teacher education questions the legitimacy of the method. The same values we ask teachers to incorporate in their Montessori classrooms we must also be able to incorporate in our teacher education.

Of course, there must be logistics. There must be standards. Even the Montessori materials have some demonstration completion. But sometimes, staying true to what we say we believe as Montessorians means being willing to acknowledge when the logistical choices we have made as adults are insufficient. No course is perfect. None of us, a hundred years later, can be assured that we, and we alone, have understood the Montessori method in its complex entirety. This is an act of faith. When we begin our teaching careers on the premise that our training was better, stronger, more authentic, more pure, we invest in our warheads instead of our tractors.

The teacher's mission has for its aim something constant and exact, bearing in mind the words, "He must grow while I diminish."

—Maria Montessori

47

Without opening your door,
You can know the whole world.

What is the very first goal of Montessori? Is it academic or is it humanitarian? Are we first teachers or first peacemakers? If all our children can read and perform complex mathematical operations, does it really matter if we've done the "peace thing"?

Part of understanding our emphases is understanding our values. Why do we put so much emphasis on reading? Because it opens other doors. Why do we put so much emphasis on math? Because it opens other doors. Because without a strong, academic foundation, students lack the skills to be successful as adults. But what kind of adults are we preparing them to be, if we are always telling them that what they know is more important than how they behave?

What comes first? When we overlook the global vision of Montessori in exchange for the academic standards in front of us, we sacrifice the heart in exchange for the mind. We can't survive with only one. We must have both to thrive. But even as embryos, our hearts come first.

We begin our peaceful classrooms with the grace and courtesy lessons. Each of the grace and courtesy lessons teaches the child how to make life more comfortable *for others.* They begin from that same humility: that we are responsible to others first. Just as there are no special tables at which we are polite to each other, grace and courtesy pervades our classrooms, becoming the foundation for the academic materials instead of some special topic limited to group time.

Likewise, the cultural materials are not just an interesting way to teach geography. They help the child to understand the vastness of our earth and universe and the great responsibility each of us shares to nurture it. They help the child to understand the vastness of human life and that same responsibility to nurture one another. In this way, the peacefulness of Montessori comes first from a dichotomous humility, that we are each tiny bits of a much larger unfolding and that our every action affects its path. We are both imperceptible and indomitable. We cannot experience that by adding sums and diagramming sentences. But we don't have to leave our classrooms to understand it.

If education is always to be conceived along the same antiquated lines of a mere transmission of knowledge, there is little to be hoped from it in the bettering of man's future.

—*Maria Montessori*

48

Mastery of the world is achieved
By letting things take their natural course.
You can not master the world by changing the natural way.

What do we call ourselves? Are we teachers? Guides? Directresses? Servants? Scientists? Saints? All the names we give ourselves, with the hope that we will better define what we do and what our role is ... none of them are as important as the choices we make with children every day.

Whatever we call ourselves, our most important work is supporting the development of each individual child. We trust that the child's development will follow that secret process and that if we get out of the way, the true nature of the child can be preserved. We want so badly to predict its path, but the direction of the child's life is seen only in the tracks it leaves. Our only choice is to watch carefully, to understand how this child's path differs from that child's. Our view is terribly clouded when we are kicking up too much of our own dust on the trail.

Observe. Then, when you're finished, observe some more. When you have made some choice, added some feature or removed some obstacle to better serve the child, observe some more. The path of the child is always there. There is nothing, nothing, we can do to stop the child from learning, from growing, from becoming an adult. But we can throw boulders on the path. The child will still climb over them and will carry with him the scrapes and bruises he endured in doing so.

Imagine the tiny sapling. Can you change its nature? Can you make it become a different kind of tree? Of course not. But you can make sure it has sufficient light. You can make sure it has rich soil and a fertile ground. You can offer it support when it needs it, just as you can remove the supports when they begin to intrude on the tree's ability to stand alone. Our support, forced beyond when it is needed, leaves scars on the trunk of the growing tree, and yet the tree insists on growing. Its environment will determine if it grows strong and upright or if it is forced to bend and twist to be assured its needs are met.

No guide, no teacher can divine the intimate needs of each pupil and the time of maturation necessary to each; but only leave the child free and all this will be revealed to us under the guidance of nature.

—*Maria Montessori*

49

To those who are good she treats as good.
To those who aren't good she also treats as good.
This is how she attains true goodness.

How much forgiveness do you offer? How much do you hope is offered to
you? Is there some point beyond which the challenging child no longer
deserves our compassion or love?

It is so hard sometimes when we want our love for the children to come
easily. We want children to have their own personalities so long as they
also listen to our directions. We want them to be feisty, to be vigorous and
spirited and joyful, except at nap time. We want them to love us as much
as we want to love them. And sometimes they don't. Sometimes our personalities clash. We don't understand one another. We grow more frustrated and more distant and less loving toward one another. Finally, we
blame the child for being unlovable.

Loving each child does not mean that the teacher has the same relationship with each child. Loving the child means doing whatever we can to
provide for that child's development. Sometimes that means admitting out
loud our limits and asking for help. Sometimes it is as simple as asking
ourselves to think of a child differently. We talk to children, and they seem
so mature, so reasonable, so capable that we forget, when they "act their
age," that they are children. It is easier, if far crueler, to assign malice to a
child than to admit negligence in ourselves.

Here is the child who can never remember to eat with his mouth closed,
whose buttery hands and running nose and slobbering mouth touches
everything in our beautiful space. Here is the child, fascinated with her own
body, whose fingers find their way into the toilet, on to the walls of the
bathroom, on to herself, and to you. Here is the child who refuses to look
in your eye when he's misbehaved. And the one who runs from you on the

playground, laughing the angrier you become. Challenging may be an understatement!

When a child is challenging, he challenges our patience. He challenges our resolve. He challenges our ability to love him nonetheless. He challenges us to grow, as teachers and nurturers, past our current limits, to deeper compassion, more tireless patience, more joyful acceptance. When we are wiser teachers for having met the challenge, it will be his gooey, dripping, snot-caked face we'll have to run after to thank.

One of the great problems facing men is their failure to realize the fact that a child possesses an active psychic life even when he cannot manifest it.

—*Maria Montessori*

50

Because they are afraid of dying,
Therefore they cannot live.

Always be prepared! There are always more materials to have available. Group activities will never take exactly the amount of time you expected. If you need them to last ten minutes, they'll almost certainly be finished in five. If you only have eight minutes before carline, group time will almost certainly need at least twenty. The day you cut fresh paper will be the day every child decides to do nine new metal insets. The day after you brag about how peacefully your classroom is progressing, chaos will reign. Always be prepared!

Wise teachers take the time to think through contingencies, yet are equally spontaneous as their children. Balancing acts take skill and luck. Teaching is no different. The skill comes in thinking through, in taking the time to prepare yourself mentally and to prepare the physical space of the environment. The luck comes in those occasional, remarkable alignments of the twenty-four or thirty-six or forty different individual planets rotating around your classroom.

When we plan, we prepare for the contingencies. When we enter the classroom, we set them in motion. No day will unfold exactly as we have expected. Nor should it. These are lives. This is life. We can teach rigidity or resilience. We can value the experience or the plan.

You can't survive in the wilderness without knowledge and grounding. Likewise, you'll not last long in the classroom without the same proactive preparation. But there will always be surprises. Give yourself up to them. If you had wanted only to accept what you had written down on some lesson plan somewhere, you shouldn't have ventured into the forest.

Giving yourself the spiritual space to change course without becoming lost allows for great adventures. We don't have the same experience of the forest if we've studied our maps but never entered the woods. Sometimes you have to stray from the path to see the most vibrant wildflowers. Just be sure you know your way back.

Freedom without organization is useless. The organization of the work, therefore, is the cornerstone of this new structure. But even that organization would be in vain without the liberty to make use of it.

—Maria Montessori

51

The Tao gives birth to all of creation.
The virtue of the Tao in nature nurtures them,
And their family give them their form.
Their environment then shapes them into completion.
That is why every creature honors the Tao and its virtue.

Each new life offers our humanity another chance. From before birth, we teach our children about the world. Will there be enough food? Will there be warmth? Will there be love?

Take the time to offer infants deep respect and understanding. We know these lives are learning, just as rigorously as their older, more articulate counterparts. We know these lives are making judgments about the world and their place within it. In the hyperconcrete state of infancy, when we cannot use words to communicate, to justify and explain, every experience the child has is more acutely tied to the lessons she will learn.

As adults, we can turn our own deaf ears and think of infants as playthings. We can stuff pacifiers into mouths when they distract us. We can close doors on cries when they keep us awake. We can play with our children when it is convenient. We can push them in their strollers, carrying them only when they need to move from one contraption to another, and focus instead on how cute their clothes are. The infant will learn. She will learn that mouths can be used to satisfy emotional needs. She will learn that parents' ears are sometimes unresponsive, even to the most anguished cries. She will learn that touch is for efficiency. She will learn that appearance outweighs experience.

Or as adults, we can listen to our infants, pay attention to the things that grab their focus, let them turn their heads away in satisfaction before we move them along. We can listen to their cries as expressions of real need: of hunger, thirst, frustration, loneliness. We can carry them in our arms instead of pushing them in their vehicles. The infant will learn. She will learn that the world is worth slowing down to attend to. She will learn that parents respond, that even when they solve the problem, she does not have to suffer alone. She will learn that touching shows love. She will learn that the process is more important than the time frame.

Our infants come to us with all the tools they need to communicate. We choose as adults to listen or to ignore. We choose to teach ourselves to understand the language of infancy or to force our infants to learn our language of efficiency. We choose to respect the impact of these first lessons learned or to overlook the opportunity in exchange for faster completion. Slow down.

The child is the spiritual builder of mankind, and obstacles to his free development are the stones in the wall by which the soul of man has become imprisoned.

—*Maria Montessori*

52

If you try to talk your way into a better life
There will be no end to your trouble.
To understand the small is called clarity.
Knowing how to yield is called strength.

If only ...

If only I had more say about which children were in my classroom. If only I had more say about which materials were purchased this year. If only my colleagues would do things as I ask. If only people didn't pay such close attention. If only people paid more attention. If only I made more money. If only I could work fewer hours.

If only ...

If only the children were a little older. If only there were fewer children in diapers. If only there were more kindergartners. If only there were more girls. If only I could keep them for that third year. If only they only came from other Montessori schools. If only our school would start an infant program. If only the elementary program was in place.

If only ...

If only my parents were more responsive. If only they came to more parent-education programs. If only they stopped undoing my work at home. If only they valued Montessori as much as I do. If only they stopped pressuring me so much. If only they visited more. If only they visited less. If only they didn't ask such difficult questions. If only they seemed to be more interested.

If only ...

If only my training had prepared me for this. If only we didn't have to worry about reporting to the state. If only I could choose my assistant. If only I could choose my hours. If only the playground had more space. If only I had a garden. If only I could go to a conference this year. If only my

school would adopt that new program I found. If only I could get the support I needed.

If only ...

Hush now.

There's work to do.

*The mind of one who does not work for that which he needs, but commands it
from others, grows heavy and sluggish.*

—Maria Montessori

53

The Tao goes in the level places,
But people prefer to take the short cuts.

Our practice is so difficult and we are so impatient. We want this Montessori thing to have worked already. We want the children to be just a bit less complicated, just a little more predictable. When the wheel doesn't roll fast enough, we try to reinvent it.

We introduce new reading schemes or a new math program. We order new blackline masters or try grouping children for lessons. We move playground time to the middle of the morning, when the children seem to be so distractible. We promote our anxious third-year students in January or introduce new toddlers to the children's house in the middle of the year.

We are so impatient. We want this Montessori thing to work *now*.

If you try to carve marble with a jackhammer, it shatters. Children are complicated. Understanding them, responding to them, serving them, takes time. Because the Montessori method respects that, it too takes time.

You have learned the structure of the classroom. You have learned the time line of three years' development. The lessons you presented to the three-year-old may not come to fruition until that child is six. Don't panic. What happens to these side paths we introduce? What happens to the new reading system? Why is it that it seems we're introducing a new one every few years? If the systems that we use, for reading, for math, for our all-important academic outcomes, are consistent with the larger structure of Montessori, they will work.

Instead of looking for the new system from without, think about the systems you are already using. Are they consistent? Are they concrete? Are you teaching children lessons in one presentation that you will unteach later on? Are your presentations reliable? Remember this is a science: if we have not offered consistent stimuli, we cannot compare the outcomes. We are teaching children not only what to learn but how to learn. If presentations are sloppy, if cards are presented vertically in some presentations and horizontally in others, if we jump too quickly to the abstract before the concrete has been internalized, we have not laid the groundwork upon which the child will build knowledge. Instead of looking for answers from someone else, appreciate the complex interreliance of the method you have already chosen. Patience, patience.

Our intervention in this marvelous process is indirect; we are here to offer this life, which came into the world by itself, the means necessary for its development, and having done that we must await this development with respect.

—Maria Montessori

54

That which is well built
Will never be torn down.
That which is well latched
Cannot slip away.

Why are so many people Montessori teachers for such a short time? Why do teachers leave Montessori schools so often? Don't we all believe the same thing?

In our hearts, maybe. At our surface, no chance.

We find Montessori because it speaks to the empty space in our teaching, because it is consistent with how we always thought children should be treated or with how we hope the world will one day work. We find Montessori because it allows us to revere childhood, or it satisfies some emotional need that traditional models did not. We find Montessori first as a set of beliefs and secondarily as a specific method to implement them. And because our beliefs are so personal, so intimate, and ultimately more dear than our allegiances to schools or methods or the name "Montessori," we find little room for compromise. We break off, find other schools or start our own, carry the One True Faith with us.

Is there common ground to be found? It depends on how deeply you want to dig. The surface of the earth is diverse, and all life relies on its own unique environment. But deep down, our differences melt away. The problem is that we have to sacrifice our individuality if we are to melt together, and few of us are willing to give up our lives on the surface for the concurrence of molten earth.

Perhaps it is enough to know that we share that core, even if we cannot survive in each other's climates. If we begin first from an acknowledgment of the beliefs we share, perhaps we can see our differences as the surface bumps they are. Life is diverse and complex. Some life will be beyond the reach of warmth in the mountains and some beyond the reach of light at the bottom of the sea. We are all nonetheless tied to this earth. In our squawking and braying and screeching, we may never speak with a single voice. But we might learn to sing together, harmonious despite our differences.

Confidences would come more easily in the years they are longer for if they were invited in the years when living was exciting and every act a great adventure.

—*Maria Montessori*

55

One who is filled with the Tao
Is like a newborn child.
Its bones are soft, its muscles are weak,
But its grip is firm and strong.

Why do we burn out? Why do we lose our fire for Montessori? Because it becomes too hard to meet our own expectations. Because we fail too often to achieve our results.

Every new year, every new child, is a new unpredictable dance. We have gotten used to the steps we think are coming. We know them better than the children do, having danced them year after year. And so we trip over lots of little toes, trying to get them to learn our rhythm. We dance mindlessly, like formal partners never looking in each other's eyes. We are frustrated when we stumble.

Watch how the young child dances. Music is heard. Bodies move. Rhythms are sometimes met. Sometimes not. Hands find the air. Feet leave the ground. There is no expectation that the dance will be fluid, and there is only laughter if the child falls down. The child, thinking only of the music, is not distracted by her audience.

We burn out when we hold too tightly to what we want from the children and are too often disappointed when what they need from us is different. We burn out when we are more concerned with our audience than the movement of our bodies. We burn out when we are focused so much on the steps that we can't hear the music. Our spirits grow old.

Every new year, every new child offers a chance to renew those spirits, by letting go of what we want from the children and focusing instead on what they need from us. When you choose to stop dancing, hope that it is not because you no longer love the music. When you choose to stop dancing, let it be from joyous exhaustion.

Work is necessary; it can be nothing less than a passion; a person is happy in accomplishment.

—*Maria Montessori*

56

Stop talking.
Meditate in silence
Blunt your sharpness
Release your worries
Harmonize your inner light
And become one with the dust.

For such nurturing people, we can be so critical. We hurt each other blindly. We are so certain of our faith in Montessori that we forget that, like the materials, Montessori is not an abstract concept to be debated but a concrete one to be lived. We do profound damage to ourselves when we attack one another.

But it is like any faith. There are sects and traditions. There are elements that one group holds dear and another discards. We may all agree on the purpose of our faith, but we disagree on the rituals. We pick and choose the parts that speak to us most intimately and argue that the rest is not important. Because we are limited, we limit Montessori.

Is there space for difference? Certainly. As soon as we define what is the only acceptable Montessori, we limit it to only those children who fit that mold. When we acknowledge that the differences between Montessori schools are because of the different abilities of the adults in those communities, we allow for Montessori to reach the children for whom we are not personally able to serve. It is our limited ability as practitioners and not some inspired knowledge that affects what Montessori looks like in our classrooms. By necessity, we choose the elements of this immeasurably complex method that we can accomplish. The sharp distinctions between our schools are a measure of our imperfect ability. That does not give us the right to use them to cut one another.

It is difficult to say aloud that we are limited, both in our ability and in our understanding. But it is ultimately liberating. When we acknowledge the boundaries of what we know, we inherently set new goals, to travel further, to inquire more deeply, to serve a wider group of children than we currently do. When we acknowledge our boundaries, we break their hold on us. We can see over the fence.

What is the greatest sign of success for a teacher transformed? It is to be able to say, "The children are now working as if I did not exist."

—*Maria Montessori*

57

I do nothing,
And people become good by themselves.
I seek peace,
And people take care of their own problems.

There are times—as administrators, heads of schools, directors of pro-grams—that we are so overwhelmed by the expanse of responsibility that we feel the need to hold more tightly to our reigns. We tighten control.

The administrator is responsible for the program. The administrator sets expectations and holds teachers to them. The administrator makes the rules, writes the policy, and assures that it is being followed. It is lonely work. If the program succeeds, she must focus its success on the rest of the faculty. If the program fails, it is her failure alone.

There are three different responses as administrators. We can hold tighter to our control, allow it pervade every decision of the school, and be guaranteed that no action will occur without our explicit permission. We can let loose the reigns entirely, turn over school programs completely to classroom teachers, and absolve ourselves of any responsibility when prob-lems occur. Or we can find that middle space, within which we both take responsibility for the state of the school while trusting in the knowledge and expertise that our teachers bring to the classroom.

When we hold tighter, we suffocate the creativity of our teachers. We limit the new discoveries of the classroom. We draw a single, narrow path down which our school will squeeze. When we let loose, we provide no foundation. We lose the web of interreliance that makes a school more than an association of independent kingdoms. Our programs become only as strong as the resolve of individual teachers. When we support teachers without stifling them, when we create environments within which teachers can both experiment and fall safely, we provide both foundation and springboard. We offer the security of a program that makes decisions based on principles, and the compassion of a program that understands that different teachers may need different levels of support. In short, we model for our teachers that which we hope for our classrooms: we prepare environments within which our students can act as though we didn't exist.

Averting war is the work of politicians; establishing peace is the work of education.

—Maria Montessori

58

If a government is repressive,
The people become treacherous.

What happens in the school when teachers fear their administrators? Like children of repressive parents, they find ways to survive within the confines, or they leave. They ask less often for help. They draw attention only to their successes, or they focus attention only on the failures of their colleagues. They may remain longer than it is healthy, because they fear what will happen to the children if they go. Or they may leave so soon that the school comes to expect unpredictability and sees teacher turnover as a chronic, unavoidable problem.

When the children are not thriving, to whom do we look?

When the teachers are not thriving, to whom do we look?

It is not the responsibility of the child to fix the teacher. It is not the responsibility of the teacher to fix the school. When our classrooms suffer chronic, systemic problems, it is easy to blame the children. When our schools suffer chronic, systemic problems, it is easy to blame the teachers. Being "in charge" makes us more responsible for the problems, not less. Being in charge makes us accountable.

It is a difficult and lonely work to direct a school. There are no peers. If you answer to a board, they are your employers. Admitting your weaknesses may threaten your job. If you are a proprietor, you have no one to answer to. Even the teachers who enjoy your company cannot be entirely at ease with you. Find your support elsewhere. It is no more appropriate to seek security through control of teachers than it is for them to seek security through control of children.

Montessori asks teachers, even teachers of adults, to abdicate their control. Montessori asks us to stop ruling through terror and guide instead out of respect. We see the best in the child when we greet him with acceptance and guidance instead of an iron fist. We see the best in our teachers when we offer them gentle hands.

Only through freedom and environmental experience is it practically possible for human development to occur.

—*Maria Montessori*

59

Those who follow the Tao early
Will have an abundance of virtue.
When there is an abundance of virtue,
There is nothing that cannot be done.

We push out. We pull away. At the other side of a fear of force is the fear that we will not be fully loved. As teachers and as administrators we can exploit both fears. We use the threat of force as effectively as the removal of our affection to control.

We have seen those mothers, the ones who hold too tightly, the ones who mother and smother, sustaining their children's total reliance, desperately afraid that their children might be OK without them. We tsk-tsk. We whisper about how parenting is not about the parent but about the child.

Then in our interactions with other adults, we mimic this fruitless emotional debt. We really want our peers to like us, and so we give them the answers we think they want. As administrators, we don't want to disappoint our teachers by telling them no, so we make promises we cannot possibly keep and lay low when the bad news trickles down from our offices. We are so dependent on the immediate satisfaction of a life without conflict that we sacrifice authentic relationships with both adults and children.

There are logistical limits to what we can do, always. There are budgets to be met. There are responsibilities to other people. There are practical stopping points. When we fear being honest with one another about what the limits are, we don't make those limits disappear. Instead of being objective structures to work within, they become indicators of our lack of integrity as leaders. By trying to keep the love of our faculty, we lose their respect.

Schools are places of intense emotional commitment, but they are not a substitute for healthy, sustaining friendships independent of our work. Like wise mothers, we need to know both when to support our teachers and when to let them go. We need to be willing to say no when no is the right answer. Like wise mothers, we need to separate what is right for our teachers from what will make us feel more loved. Our strongest decisions as parents and as administrators do not rely on the love we hope we receive. Our strongest decisions are the ones that provide an environment within which we can all thrive, separate yet interreliant, loving yet able to stand alone.

What advice can we give to mothers? Their children need to work at an interesting occupation: they should not be helped unnecessarily, nor interrupted, once they have begun to do something intelligent.

—Maria Montessori

60

Governing a large country
Is like frying small fish.
Too much poking spoils the meat.

Remember what to do after you've turned a lesson over to the child?

Observe unobtrusively.

Hands off.

The material is self-correcting if we allow it to be. The child learns from her mistakes more than from our interference.

When we insist on re-presenting before the child has had the opportunity to correct herself, we steal from her the chance to stand apart from us. We teach her implicitly that unless she is exactly what we have prescribed for her to be, she is lacking.

We instill a fear of failure instead of a confidence of ability. While we believe we are helping, we teach a very different lesson. In helping, we have taken the child's opportunity to experience self-reliance.

Hands off.

We correct *intentional* error. That means we have to have provisions for the fallout of *unintentional* error. We have to have the emotional reserve to remain calm when the glass pitcher falls from the child's hands. We have to have the equipment to clean up the messes. We have to have enough carrots for when the child has peeled one to oblivion and has nothing left to cut. The noisiest missteps are the ones we weren't prepared for. Recognize that part of the first time a child uses a material independently is our observation of that use. If you can see the mistake about to happen, you can respond to it more calmly, even when you have allowed it to occur. On the contrary, if your attention ends when you step away from the work, you are distracted, interrupted, or startled if the child is unable yet to complete it without error. Be responsive without being interfering. Too much poking spoils the fish.

An adult who does not understand that a child needs to use his hands and does not recognize this as the first manifestation of an instinct for work can be an obstacle to the child's development.

—*Maria Montessori*

61

Large countries should desire to protect and help people,
And small countries should desire to serve others.
Both large and small countries benefit greatly from humility.

There are so many people to care for in Montessori. We are driven to care for the children, to nurture relationships with their parents, to serve each other as teachers and practitioners. There is always someone else who could benefit from our service.

Sometimes the person whom service can greatest benefit is the person who is so focused on helping others. It can be harder to ask for help than to offer it.

In learning to be humble, in learning to serve others before ourselves, we must also have the capabilities for service. Our ducks must be in their row. If you lack the emotional stamina and the reserves to share your spirit with others, there will be nothing left for your own sustenance.

Where do we build our reserves? They are not built in the number of materials we have presented or the handouts we've printed out. They are not built through busywork. They are built when we take the time to reflect on our relationships with other people, when we find the space in our conflicts to understand the commonalities between us. Our spiritual needs cannot be met through stuff. They are met in quiet, undistracted moments.

We focus on busywork to avoid reflection. We build walls of competence-proving papers around us to avoid facing the very real, always present fear that we may not be as competent as teachers as we seem. We all question whether we're doing enough. We all question whether we are enough. We all pretend not to.

The busywork may be necessary. So often, though, we hold forth the things of our lives as though they are the purpose of our lives. We present the documentation of evidence that we have been doing what we were meant to as teachers, when the classrooms can speak for themselves. And in focusing on the paperwork, we miss invaluable opportunities to share the language of our classrooms. Yes, the busywork may be necessary, but as a necessary afterthought to work done well, not as a substitute for the work itself.

We cannot know the consequences of suffocating a spontaneous action at the time when the child is just becoming active; perhaps we suffocate life itself.

—Maria Montessori

62

When a new leader takes office,
Don't give him gifts and offerings.
These things are not as valuable
As teaching him about the Tao.

Our structures and hierarchies are endlessly important to us. We find comfort in knowing our role. And occasionally, we find comfort in reminding others of it!

We have all experienced changes in leadership. Maybe it was another teacher who was asked to coordinate other colleagues. Maybe it was a new head of school. There is a push, in these times of change, to influence our leaders, to let them know how we do things here or perhaps to let them know how we'd rather do things here. We are threatened by the uncertainty. We might be insulted by the choice of person.

The lead dog may have the best view, but he lacks the warmth of companions around him. When leaders come into new positions, they, too, fear what will happen. Even in their confidence, they rely on others to validate their new position.

Offer kindness to leadership. You may feel the need to show him how capable you are. You may see the opportunity to get in good with the boss. There will be times, almost necessarily, when this person will be in the uncomfortable position of asking you to change something that you want to do. It is easy, in preparation for these predictable disagreements, to want to distinguish ourselves with our leaders, to protect ourselves from the potential attack. These motivations separate us from our real work both as Montessori teachers and as members of adult communities. When we build relationships with others based first on our self-interest, we create only a short-term protection. Real security comes from developing authentic relationships with our colleagues, peers, and leaders alike, in which we can acknowledge that none of us is "finished." We are traveling together.

School leaders—be they administrators, lead teachers, or heads of school—are isolated. Offer them companionship. School leaders are fallible. Offer them forgiveness. School leaders are human. Offer them humanity.

If help and salvation are to come, they can only come from the children, for the children are the makers of men.

—Maria Montessori

63

Act by not acting;
Do by not doing.
Enjoy the plain and simple.
Find that greatness in the small.
Take care of difficult problems
While they are still easy;
Do easy things before they become too hard.

Our Montessori environments are so different from the rest of the world. There are times when our work seems futile. For every Montessori child we teach peace, there are ten, a hundred, a thousand more in our communities who are taught hatred. For each humanity we preserve through our work, the world around us destroys a hundred thousand more. What use is it to serve twenty if there are twenty thousand unserved?

Here is a basic: Each child's life is exceptionally valuable, singularly rare, priceless, and irreplaceable. Each child. Most of our children come from families with some advantages, if only that their parents or guardians knew to find them a Montessori school. It is easy sometimes to think that we are working with the wrong children. We are serving the children who need us the least.

Even the blessed life can be difficult to the one who lives it.

Each child we serve, in turn, learns to serve others. Each child whose life we touch in turn touches others. Ours is not work to be accomplished in a lifetime but across lifetimes. When it appears fruitless, when we are daunted, know that we are accomplishing the great task through that series of small acts.

Each of us, too, is exceptionally valuable, singularly rare, priceless, and irreplaceable. Each of us. We are together painting an enormous canvas. Each brushstroke counts. It may take many lifetimes to complete the work. It may never be completed, brushed over by new artists, tweaked by cultural whims. But what a masterpiece in the making.

We could study a child from every angle and know everything about him from the cells of his body to the countless details of his every operation and we would still not perceive his ultimate goal, that is, the adult he is to become.

—*Maria Montessori*

64

Prevent problems before they arise.
Take action before things get out of hand.

When does the school day end? When the children go home? When the teachers go home? When the lights are out? Oh, no. Not then. Ours is a persistent practice. It doesn't matter if there are children there or not. Somewhere, the children are growing and changing. We are always preparing for their return.

A simple observation: The unprepared environment is chaos. The prepared environment is peace.

A far more complex question: What exactly is this prepared environment? If we have set the materials, scrubbed the shelves, consulted our manuals, stockpiled the carrots, isn't that prepared?

Yes, but there's more!

OK. If we have reviewed our observations, refilled the paper, sharpened the pencils, turned in our reports, returned the parents' phone calls, isn't that prepared?

Yes, but there's more!

OK. OK. If we have reflected on each child, written in our journals, prepared new cultural materials, taken time to discuss issues with our colleagues, made our lists of presentations we'd like to get to tomorrow, isn't *that* prepared?

Yes, but...well, you know.

There is always more. When problems arise, they point out to us just what we forgot to consider. When chaos breaks out in our classrooms, they remind us of how much more there was to do. We are given the gift of peace to remind us that it's possible, and the gift of unexpected chaos to remind us of what we forgot to expect. Sometimes, we will have done enough, but there's always more.

Either education contributes to a movement of universal liberation by showing the way to defend and raise humanity or it becomes like one of those organs which have shriveled up by not being used during the evolution of the organism.

—*Maria Montessori*

65

The ancient Masters
Who understood the way of the Tao,
Did not educate people, but made them forget.

Montessori classrooms present children the world. Everything that we know, every scientific discovery or complex reaction … we have found some way to make them concrete, specific, and understandable to the child. We are filled with facts, from our youngest children, classifying the kingdoms of life to our oldest, charting the universe.

We know that our role as Montessori teachers is to turn responsibility back to the child, not to answer all the questions but to give the child the tools to find her answers herself. We do that well often enough. Take care, though, that we don't do it so well that we teach the child that all questions have answers.

There are wondrous unexplainables that happen around us every day. There are wondrous explainables that happen as well, no less remarkable for their scientific justification. In taking time for the wondrous, we remind the child that not all questions have answers, nor do they need them.

What made that bird land just so on the playground fence? Why is this blade of grass so thick and another so thin? How can the paint that feels so smooth and cool and soft in my hand become so crisp and dry and sharp? Why do oranges taste so much sweeter when my eyes are closed? There are answers we can know, but in focusing on the answers, we rush through the wonder.

We think that this wonder is unique to early childhood, that elementary and middle school students are too savvy for awe, too kinetic for silence. We think wonder is something we grow out of and so we cherish it in the young child. Perhaps it is not that we have outgrown our wonder but that we have stifled it under our sophisticated agendas. Sit quietly one day. Put aside your clipboard and notes. Put aside your quest for answers. Watch the children. Whatever age they are. Watch them without purpose. Remember who they were when you met them or who you were at their age. Wonder may not be that far away.

Our first teacher, therefore, will be the child himself, or rather the vital urge with the cosmic laws that lead him unconsciously.

—*Maria Montessori*

66

Rivers and seas are rulers
Of the streams and hundreds of valleys
Because of the power of their low position.

Have you ever lain on your back and stared into the night sky? Surrounded by the sounds of our earth, we are aware of how very small, how very insignificant we are. Try to count the stars. In counting them up, you'll notice the ones you overlooked. In counting those, you'll realize there are more.

What is it that drives our awe when we are lying on our backs? Is it the magnitude? Or is it that, within that magnitude, there are endless, boundless possibilities, beyond our imaginations, beyond our conception? Conscious of all the futures that our own choices have made impossible, we are that much more aware of the infinite potential above us.

In each child is that same infinite potential.

Staring at the stars is a concrete experience of our insignificance. We are prone, helpless, in awe. How can we capture that experience and bring it with us when we are upright, staring down at children instead of up into the sky? It is much harder when we are taller, stronger, older, when we can touch or lift or restrain the universes in front of us. It is much more difficult when the universe talks back.

But the universe of the child is no more finite in its potential. It too contains boundless possibilities beyond our imaginations, beyond our conception. And in a far smaller container! What is more wondrous—the magnitude of infinite possibility that is presented to us in the stars, or that same infinite possibility in the tiny life we can hold in our hands? What requires greater care—the universe we cannot possibly contain or the one we can destroy with our careless attempts to define its capacity?

In watching these lives, we glimpse the shadow of infinity. In serving them, we acknowledge our own finiteness before that potential. Our choices may have been made, our boundaries drawn, but in the humble service to the child, we are reconnected to that universe, our walls broken down. In our humility before her potential, we too are unbound.

The most urgent task facing educators is to come to know this unknown child and to free it from all entanglements.

—Maria Montessori

67

There are three jewels that I cherish:
Compassion, simplicity, and patience.

Simplicity. Patience. Compassion.

Simplicity: the casting aside of our pretentiousness. In focusing on the core, we can distinguish what is essential and what is superfluous.

Patience: the casting aside of our annoyances. In granting time, we see things as they are now rather than how they are lacking.

Compassion: the casting aside of our judgments. In embracing how we are the same, we replace our selfish agendas with reunion and peace.

Let these be the foundations of your teaching. Let them be the foundation for your learning. If we build our classrooms on pretensions, they are bound to deceive. If we build our classrooms on annoyances, they are bound to repress. If we build our classrooms on judgment, they are bound to condemn.

If we build our classrooms on simplicity, they are free to find our common soil. If we build our classrooms on patience, they are free to grow at their own pace. If we build our classrooms on compassion, they are free to wind together, climbing higher for the support we offer each other.

What a garden!

The child has other powers than ours, and the creation he achieves is no small one. It is everything.

—*Maria Montessori*

68

The best leaders
Become servants of their people.

When young children play, who wins? They all do! It is only after we have taught them about winners and losers, best and worst, that they too begin to distinguish between who was faster, stronger, more able.

When our schools play, who wins? Do we think of our teaching as loyal to one school, one teacher-education program, one affiliation? In distinguishing ourselves as "best," we shame others as the losers. We have forgotten how to play as children do.

This is not just within our Montessori community but between us and other teachers as well. When we set Montessori aside, make it unique and untouchable and prestigious, we create competition where there could be collaboration. When we think of ourselves as the sole method in the service of children, we make ourselves the "winners" at the expense of the child.

Just as there are children who will learn earlier to place one hand in front of the other across the monkey bars, just as there are children who will learn earlier how to pump their legs to take their swings aloft, there will be developments, evolutions, discoveries that make us more effective. Some of them were Montessori's. Some were not. If we continue to set ourselves aside, to pin blue ribbons to our own boastful chests, we lose the chance to play together. We lose the chance to learn from other people's practice and to share with them ours. We exclude players to the sidelines who could otherwise enhance the game.

Play as children do. There are fewer gold medals, but the game is so much more fun.

Man, as a spiritual being, has been left to the mercy of outer circumstances and is on the way to becoming a destroyer of his own constructions.

—*Maria Montessori*

69

When equal forces meet in battle,
Victory will go to the one
That enters with the greatest sorrow.

Who hasn't found herself in a power struggle with a child? We avoid them. We know we can't win, and yet every once in a while (or more often than that!) we nonetheless find ourselves waiting to see who is more stubborn, more obstinate, more inflexible. When did we decide that one of our goals was immovable pigheadedness?

Avoiding power struggles is one of the ways in which we offer the child our respect. Our lives in Montessori classrooms are not about making rules to be lived within but understanding life abundant. When we find ourselves in a test of wills with a child, we have stopped living in exchange for being right or being indisputable or being absolute. We don't want to back down for the other lessons it will teach the child. We are afraid to admit that we don't actually care so much about the thing at hand as we do about being obeyed.

Yield. There is nothing to be gained in the conflict. Even if you cannot surrender the outcome, yield the battle. Acknowledge that the debate at hand has ceased to be about action and has instead disintegrated into stagnant stalemate. It is no longer about your wishes or the child's but about who is controlling whom. If you are in a power struggle, you have already surrendered control.

When the children have lost their self-restraint, what do we do? We help them to express themselves more clearly. We help them to articulate their concerns to each other. We help them to seek resolution. When as adults we lose our self-restraint, what do we do? We pretend it hasn't happened. We chalk it up to the mulishness of the child. We dig our heels in deeper. Why can't we ask for the same help we would offer two children?

It is not about who is the adult and who is the child. In finding mediation, particularly when we're in power struggles with children, we offer the children a model for peaceful consensus. We assure the children through authentic action and not just rhetoric that we really will respect them. We abdicate authority in exchange for peace, and in doing so give ourselves and the children the experience of discovering resolution.

We must, therefore, quit our roles as jailers and instead take care to prepare an environment in which we do as little as possible to exhaust the child with our surveillance and instruction.

—*Maria Montessori*

70

If you want to know me,
Look inside your heart.

We were children once. We had teachers and schools and had to deal with adults. We grew and had some more. We grew and grew and grew and somehow stopped being children and somehow stopped being students and somehow became the adults other children would have to deal with. But swear it to be true, we were children once.

We found Montessori because of the experiences we had as children and as students, for the way we dealt with adults and the way they dealt with us. For some of us, those experiences were so positive that we were committed to repeating them for other children. For some of us, those experiences were so hurtful that we were committed to assuring no child would suffer them again. Whether we have come to Montessori because our childhoods made us feel vast or because our childhoods made us feel insignificant, we are here now because of the children we were.

When you are facing the child whose heart is open and overflowing, find yourself in that child. Remember the adult you loved dearly. Respond as you wish that adult had responded to you. When you are facing the child whose heart is locked away, find yourself in that child, too. Remember the adult who you feared. Respond as you wish that adult had responded to you.

One day, we opened our eyes and found ourselves bound to our alarm clocks and timetables and responsibilities and checkbooks. One day, we opened our eyes and found ourselves with spouses and mortgages and children of our own. One day, we opened our eyes and discovered that, slowly, imperceptibly, we had stopped being children. What a immeasurable disservice to the children we once were if we forget what it felt like then. Simply because we have stopped being children does not mean we never were. Swear it to be true, we were children once.

The child is no greater mystery than your own heart.

We must learn how to call upon the man which lies dormant in the soul of a child.

—*Maria Montessori*

71

Knowing you don't know is wholeness
Thinking you know is a disease

Of the many challenges to being a Montessori teacher, perhaps the one we struggle with most is the voluntary abdication of our "teacherness." We were called to "teach." We trained in "teacher" colleges or "teacher"-education programs. Our students and their parents and our colleagues in other schools all call us "teachers." And yet, we have chosen a method of "teaching" that asks us to put aside all the cultural and social implications of that word.

In our culture, to be a "teacher" is to be an authority, to be the person to whom questions are asked, through whom questions get answered. It means you get the big desk. It means you get to be in the spotlight, at the front of the room, in the adult chair. In our culture, to be a "teacher" means confidence and control.

When we chose Montessori, we agree to give that back over, to make ourselves less central, more obscure. We chose to be a catalyst to our ultimate uselessness. We hasten our futility. It is a distinctly vulnerable position. Our response can be to hold fast to the things we can control, to micromanage the parts of the classroom that will not leave us. We become impossibly stubborn about the presentation of a particular material. We assign arbitrary tasks to our assistants because we are *the teacher*. We speak of Montessori as a practice that we have already mastered.

When we finish our Montessori training, we are not finished. When we have finished our first year of teaching, we are still not finished. When we have been made lead teacher, we are still not finished. When we coordinate the program, direct the school, teach the other teachers, we are still not finished.

When we believe we are finished, we are finished.

When we are finished, we have closed ourselves to any other growth. There is no more work to do. The work of the classroom is to leave us. It is easy to find security in the things that won't. But everything is changing, all the time. Our work is to keep pace.

It is solely from a child that a man is born. An adult cannot take part in this work.

—Maria Montessori

72

The Master knows herself but is not arrogant.
She loves herself but also loves others.
This is how she is able to make appropriate choices.

Is Montessori a cult?

Sometimes.

When we close our minds to critical thought and trade our independence for blind adherence, it is. When we memorize manuals without thinking about purposes, it is. When we defend arbitrary practices as being "for the child," it is. When we defend our own lack of consistency as "following the child," it is. When we complain that the people who challenge us "just don't understand Montessori," it is. When we use Montessori to exclude, diminish, and disdain others, it is.

There is so much precision in our work. The exact placement of the materials does matter. The thoughtful preparation of the environment is essential. In a practice that is so focused on exactness, it is easy to apply those same rules to our human interactions. It is easy to forget that Montessori is not about implementing a specific method separate from your own mind or spirit but about a life practice of integrating what we have been taught with what we know.

This method is not strengthened by blind obedience but by thoughtful, mindful preparation. If you choose to present a material, it should not be just that it comes next on the sequence but because you have considered the child, considered the material, and concluded that the match is right. When we make policy, it should not be that we've seen it done in another school or that a school consultant told us to do it but because we believe that the policy will make us better able to serve our communities and satisfy our values. When we interact with each other, we can choose to goad each other with critiques about how we didn't do it that way in *our* training, or we can receive each other as valuable contributors to each of our practices. We can trade in our cult for community and exchange our adamancy for love.

An educational method which cultivates and protects the inner activities of the child is not a question which concerns merely the school or the teachers; it is a universal question.

—Maria Montessori

73

The nets of Heaven are wide,
But nothing escapes its grasp.

How in the world is it that Montessori classrooms can present the entire universe and endless details, facts, and definitions to children in the course of a few years in the space of a single classroom?

The net we cast is tied with a single thread: that every part of the universe, great or small, present in our hands or imagined in our minds is connected. The thin lines we are able to see define the holes of the web, and while there may be more blank space than tangible silk, it remains complete.

This is Montessori's global vision. Not the specific presentation of a few great lessons but the impact of the lessons themselves. We take the time to build the child's understanding of her tools so that she can in turn discover the universe on her own. The tools are the practical skills—coordinating our bodies, knowing how to read, understanding measurement, and the like. We construct the web, like the cording around an archaeological site, then let the child dig deeper. The holes may not all be active at once. There are some that may never be touched. But the gridwork is there.

Our challenge, then, is in finding the silk, designing the structure, understanding which threads are necessary and which are superfluous. It is no small task indeed, and we only have two legs! Even the smallest spiders have six! The web of our classroom structures is equally fragile. It can be torn. Gaps appear. When they do, we cannot disregard them. If there is a hole in the web, it must be repaired or the entire structure is in peril. Our classrooms fail to provide those tools if there are weak points

in the structure. The children cannot hang on to a shaky thread.
When we secure the web, we present the universe in its holes.

The child should love everything he learns. Whatever is presented to him must be made beautiful and clear. Once this love has been kindled, all problems confronting the educationalist will disappear.

—*Maria Montessori*

74

Those who harm others
Are like inexperienced boys
Trying to take the place of a great lumberjack.

We want so much to protect these children, these lives that have unfolded before us since infancy, whom we love as our own. But we can't control their futures. Lives will change. Great acts of terror and small acts of unkindness will affect them, no matter how peaceful the communities we have prepared for them are.

We cannot control the future any more than we can change the past. The only moments we can touch are the ones before us right now. Terrible things will happen. We can respond by trying to build higher walls, thicker doors, deeper moats, but still terrible things will happen. We make promises that cannot possibly be kept, that we will always be there or that we can always keep the children safe. Then, when those promises fail as they inevitably will, the child is betrayed both by the world that has hurt him and the adult who, in her desperation to protect, has deceived him.

Our bodies are organic shells. Our spirits will cast them aside, sometimes when we're ready and sometimes when we're not.

All we can offer is this: No matter what happens, and many whats will happen, I will love you. No matter what global attacks or private sufferings, I will love you. No matter if we can hold each other or if we are miles or lifetimes away from each other, I will love you. I cannot offer you protection, but I can bring comfort. I cannot change the future, but every moment, in this moment and now this one and now this one, I will love you.

There is great solace in love.

The children are almost like saints or godly and I didn't want to spoil it by saying anything wrong. They are so innocent, I didn't want to mislead them.

—Maria Montessori

75

When people become rebellious,
The government has become too intrusive.
Only those who do not cling to their life can save it.

What a tricky thing, these parents are! Are they our clients? Our partners? Our community? Our adversaries? Here's one thing for sure: they are more important, no matter how wonderful or inspirational or fulfilling you are as a teacher, in the lives of their children, than you ever can or hope to be.

You may spend forty hours a week with a child. You may spend more time than that! You may be with a child more often than their parents are, involved in more life lessons, and still you will not influence them as much as the presence or absence of their very first love will. Sometimes, we take comfort in this news: we blame parents for the problems we're having at school or accuse them for not being enough for their children. Sometimes, the news is daunting: we want to think that we can overcome the challenges the child has, that we can fix her world by being the parent she doesn't have at home.

Whether the parent is present or not, whether the parent is involved or negligent, whether the parent is alive or dead, you cannot take the parent's place.

The lesson then is to acknowledge the immense and immeasurable influence of parents, even in their absence, and respond for the child. Our roles as advocates are not to be taken lightly. In serving children, we serve their parents and families, too. That means acknowledging that, whether we like it or not, the child loves the parent. Our every interaction with that parent then must come first from a concession to that love. If we greet parents with disdain, if we criticize them and ostracize them and exclude their input, we insult the child. If we greet parents as our betters, we defer to the love the child feels. We can build relationships there, offer input and help them to serve their children, but it must be as an advisor, not a decision maker. If our guidance is offered with a heavy hand, we create distance with the people we are most trying to reach. It is not the parents' responsibility to prove to us that they are doing enough for their children. That the child loves the parent is always enough to mandate our reverence to that union, no matter how dysfunctional or damaging or unworkable that union may be.

That the child loves the parent is always enough to evoke our compassion for them both.

Children become like the things they love.

—Maria Montessori

76

The living are soft and yielding;
The dead are rigid and stiff
The rigid and stiff will be broken.
The soft and yielding will overcome.

From where does our resilience come? That inner drive to keep coming back, year after year, challenge after challenge? It comes from our willingness to change, to grow, and to bend. The trees that can bear the heaviest winds are not the ones with the sturdiest trunks ... those snap in two. The trees that survive have deep roots and pliant trunks. They endure through their flexibility.

Change will happen. Teachers will change. Parents will change. Schools change systems and materials. Policies change. We can concentrate only on our melancholy and remind one another of how it used to be better. Or we can find, even in changing winds, our deep roots.

There are some things about which we can be uncompromising. These are our roots. Kindness toward children. Kindness toward one another. Compassion. These are the qualities that guide us, even when we are compromising. We can raise concerns without sinking to unkindness. We can disagree without distancing ourselves. And when it is time to go, we can do so with compassion.

How do you affect the thick-trunked tree? It is growing as it is growing and as it has always grown. You can cut it. You can scar its body. You can uproot it. It is only by damaging what the tree already is that you can change its direction.

How do you affect the green sprout? Move the water. Move the light. The growing life moves toward its sustenance. We are all that way. We move toward the things that nurture us, just as we grow thicker skins when we have been scarred.

When we are willing to bend, we can find our light, our water, our nurture, without so much struggle. When we are willing to bend, we find our needs are met, sometimes because we have reached out to others and sometimes because they have wound their ways to us.

There will be times when your needs are not met. It is in the roughest climate that our roots grow deeper, that the parts of us that can be compromised fall away, when we can see what are our essentials. Be grateful to the drought.

A teacher, by his passive attitude, removes from the children the obstacle that is created by his own activity and authority.

—Maria Montessori

77

Who is able to give to the needy from their excess?
Only some one who is following the way of the Tao.
This is why the Master gives
Expecting nothing in return.

Is humility an inherent trait? There is little humility in the toddler room, just big personalities capable of doing everything on their own, with little awareness that anyone else might be in their paths and even less to what has been left in their wakes. Humility is the consolation prize of struggle. There is some time when each of us faces challenges that we are unexpectedly unable to meet. We are humbled by the experience. There is some time when our confidence, our competence, our capability, is not enough. We are humbled.

Humility comes from the world continually reminding us of our insignificance, and pride from our refusal to learn that lesson.

We all have our expectations for our classrooms. We all hope that they will be successful, that the parents will be happy, that the children will thrive. Even when we don't expect it, we appreciate the gratitude that is offered to us, the kind words from a colleague or the thoughtful notes from families.

Acting to garner the acclaim your success may bring you is a complicated equation. You have to do something. That something has to affect someone else. That effect has to be so great, so positive, so lasting that someone else notices it. That notice has to be so focused that the person shares it with others. That audience has to feel so strongly about it that it voices its acclaim to you. Whew! So many steps just to get to the thank-you you had hoped to receive.

Wise teaching acts simply. You do something because it will benefit the child. If it works, the child is better off. If it does not, you try again. Act simply. The math is so much easier.

The child is not an inert being who owes everything he can do to us, as if he were an empty vessel that we have to fill.

—Maria Montessori

78

Water is the softest and most yielding substance
Yet nothing is better than water
For overcoming the hard and rigid ...

How is it that the children, who are so vulnerable, so easily influenced, so easy to control end up with such a profound influence on our sturdy adult lives? It is in their vulnerability that they evoke our compassion.

We see in children the lives we could have had. We laugh with their discovering. We suffer with their sadness. Like the thick silt at the mouth of the river, our adult lives are the hard stones that have fallen out of our childhood's water. Our childhoods moved on, and we are left with the sediment.

What luck, then, that children allow us to be with them every day! What grace is offered to us, to let their water run over our dense hardness. What a gift that even the most callous stone cannot resist it.

The roughest water will have the most noticeable influence. It may be the gentle flow that turns us to soft river rock, but those large, coarse stones are faster freed by racing water. We will not survive it unchanged. But nor should we want to.

When we are stuck in our solidity, we need to find water. Go downstairs from the office and observe the children. Push aside the dams we create in interfering with the children and observe with stillness. Take no notes. Just be in the water. These small moments can revive us. When we are in the water too long, we get used to its feeling. We forget it surrounds us. We start thinking of what else we need to do. Attend to the things that need attending but find time for brief dips without agenda. Their lives flow with laughter, with sadness, with simple concentration and unfettered chaos. They flow and flow and flow.

Let us start with one very simple reflection: the child, unlike the adult, is not on his way to death. He is on his way to life.

—*Maria Montessori*

79

Therefore the Master
Does what she knows is right,
And makes no demands of others.
A virtuous person will do the right thing,
And persons with no virtue will take advantage of others.

There will be more times than any of us want to admit when we will make poor choices, when we will hurt children, when our missteps will send us reeling to the ground. There will be more times than any of us want to admit when we will fail to keep our promises to ourselves, to the children, and to this practice.

These are failures. Failures of resolve. Failures of experience. Failures of knowledge. Failures of resiliency. Failures of spirit. Failures of compassion. There will be times when there was nothing we could have done to prevent our mistakes. There will be times when the number of ways in which we have gone wrong will terrify us.

Or not. We may choose not to pay attention to our failures. We may chose to acknowledge them only in others and to dismiss the impact our mistakes have had. We may even revel in blame and finger-pointing, finding fault with parents and other teachers, knowing that if only that other person had not behaved that way, we would not be in this situation right now. There is comfort in condemnation, but there is opportunity in failure.

It can be easier to offer apology to a child than to an adult. The child, in his infinite love, will offer you immediate grace. The adult, in his glass house of faultlessness, may berate before forgiving, if he forgives at all. Those denigrations benefit him. They keep him from facing his own failures. So be it. Sincere apology is a self-blessing. Sincere apology is an outward way to offer yourself grace, to step forward out of failure and move on.

When we open our eyes courageously to our own failures, we allow ourselves to learn from them. We create space for reunion with the people we have hurt. We accept that we have acted unwisely, and in doing so, show wisdom.

This is the bright new hope for mankind. Not reconstruction, but help for the constructive work that the human soul is called upon to do, and to bring to fruition; a work of formation which brings out the immense potentialities with which children, the sons of men, are endowed.

—*Maria Montessori*

80

Let people enjoy the simple technologies,
Let them enjoy their food,
Let them make their own clothes.

The child finds joy in work. We repel it. The child finds contentment through her hands. We look for ways for our responsibilities, our have-tos, and our work, to go faster, more efficiently, with more use. The child works without tiring. We look forward to sleeping in and napping often.

All of our efforts to distance ourselves from labor bring us farther and farther from one another, farther and farther from reunion. This is true too of our relationships with children. We want them to be simple, efficient, reliable. We don't want to have to sweat too much to build them or maintain them.

If a thing is to last, it takes an investment of time, of spirit, and of labor. This too is true of our relationships with children. If we think they should come easy, we overlook the intense complexity of each child. If we think they should be reliable, we underestimate the breadth and width of the child's life. We think smaller packages are somehow less complicated.

When we have spent the day laboring with our bodies, relying on our hands and muscles to plant a garden or build a tree house, our exhaustion is deeper, our satisfaction more acute. We sleep more soundly because our bodies and our spirits have been satisfied. When we have spent our time with children, laboring with our spirits, relying on sharp observation and deep compassion to plant a relationship or build trust, again, our bodies and our spirits are satisfied. We find ourselves with a more sincere understanding of the child both because we have taken the time to know him and because we have done so with his tools.

The child is always working. We choose to work against her or work with her. In lessons and in love, we can choose to work against the child or with the child. The more satisfying work takes time, spirit, and labor. The easier path leaves us restless. Sleep deeply.

To care for, and keep awake, the guide within every child is therefore a matter of first importance.

—*Maria Montessori*

81

True words do not sound beautiful;
Beautiful-sounding words are not true.
Wise men don't need to debate;
Men who need to debate are not wise.

What has brought you to this practice? What has brought you to this book? Are you looking for authority? For validation? For guidance?

You are your only guide.

There will be people who will forge paths for you. There will be teachers and colleagues and parents and children who will help to shine a light down the dark wooded path. There will be companions who will walk with you, some briefly and some for a lifetime, but every step is yours.

You are your only guide.

Listen in your heart. If a book or a poem or a song or a piece of advice speaks to you, it is only because it helped you to translate your own heart's language. We are still like that soft wax of childhood. We can be pressed and pushed. We can change our shape by the manipulation of the people around us. But in the end, we have the same density, the same volume, the same capacity we had before they touched us.

You are your only guide.

We share some purpose in this divine beautiful chaotic unfolding. Some of us will find it early. Some of us will never realize we are even looking. There are truths. Simplicity. Patience. Compassion. Offer them to yourself as readily as you offer them to the children before you. Offer them to the children as readily as you offer them to yourself. It's all the same in the end.

You are your only guide.
Namaste.

Man is a sculptor of himself, urged by a mysterious inner force to the attainment of an ideal determined form.

—*Maria Montessori*

978-1-58348-298-8
1-58348-298-9